BUILT,
NOT
BORN

BUILT, NOT BORN

A SELF-MADE BILLIONAIRE'S
NO-NONSENSE GUIDE FOR ENTREPRENEURS

TOM GOLISANO
FOUNDER OF PAYCHEX

with **MIKE WICKS**

HarperCollins
Leadership

AN IMPRINT OF HarperCollins

Published by HarperCollins Leadership, an imprint of HarperCollins Focus LLC.

Any internet addresses, phone numbers, or company or product information printed in this book are offered as a resource and are not intended in any way to be or to imply an endorsement by HarperCollins Leadership, nor does HarperCollins Leadership vouch for the existence, content, or services of these sites, phone numbers, companies, or products beyond the life of this book.

This book is written as a source of information only. The information contained herein should by no means be considered a substitute for the advice, decisions, or judgment of the reader's financial or other professional advisor. Thus, neither the publisher nor the author assumes liability of any kind for any losses that may be sustained as a result of applying the methods suggested in this book, and any such liability is hereby expressly disclaimed.

ISBN 978-1-4002-1760-1 (eBook)
ISBN 978-1-4002-1755-7 (HC)

Printed in the United States of America
20 21 22 23 24   LSC   10 9 8 7 6 5 4 3 2 1

CONTENTS

CONTENTS

CONTENTS

CONTENTS

CONTENTS

DEDICATION

This book is dedicated to the original entrepreneurs who helped build Paychex. They took the risks, and they made it work.

Phil Wehrheim, Syracuse
Robert Sebo, Cleveland
Charles Wollmer, Miami
Robert Beegen, Detroit
Michael LoCurto, Los Angeles
James Wayman, Boston
Thomas Tracy, Washington, DC
Kevin Dugan, Philadelphia
Ronald Nowak, Atlanta
Ronald Raab, Denver
Thomas Beatty, Seattle
Willis Hall, Phoenix
Jack Hartland, Houston
Gene Polisseni, Cincinnati
Gloria Austin Golisano, New York City
Henry Knapp, New Orleans
Thomas Kubiak, Systems Engineer
Gerald Reynell, Buffalo
G. Thomas Clark, Chief Financial Officer
. . . and Marty Mucci, CEO, along with the 15,500 dedicated people who currently work for Paychex and who service our 670,000 clients and shareholders.

ACKNOWLEDGMENTS

I am grateful to the many people who have helped turn *Built, Not Born* into a reality. I'm especially thankful for all the entrepreneurs out there who launch new businesses every day. They are the bedrock of the American economy and the inspiration for this book.

I am immensely thankful to all the people I have worked with over the years at Paychex. Most of the lessons I share in this book were learned during my time building the company and working alongside so many talented individuals.

I'd like to thank my coauthor, Mike Wicks of Kevin Anderson and Associates, for his tireless efforts. His commitment and passion for the project were inspiring. His contribution to the content and his ability to find my voice helped make the book both readable and accessible.

To Steve Pigeon, my friend and advisor, who worked with us every day during the writing process and whose contribution was invaluable: I'd like to thank you for always being there for me.

Thank you, Kevin Anderson, for bringing Mike Wicks to me and for introducing me to Celeste Fine, my literary agent. Your guidance throughout the publishing process helped me navigate my way through the world of editors, agents, and publishers.

My heartfelt thanks go to Marty Mucci, Blake Gable, and Larry Quinn for reading each draft to ensure accuracy, and for making so many useful suggestions and notations. Your support helped make this a book of which I am truly proud.

To Naomi Whittel, without whom I may never have found Kevin Anderson and Associates and Mike in the first place: your marketing insights and wisdom, your ongoing support and commitment to this book, and, of course, your friendship mean a lot to me.

My special thanks to Matt Ray for his specific help in writing the section on understanding the various legal business structures companies can adopt.

My thanks to my very talented literary agent, Celeste Fine, and to my publisher, HarperCollins Leadership.

PREFACE

There is a difference between the business principles taught in academic institutions and those learned over many years of actually running a business. Both experiences have their place and value, and a good entrepreneur can learn from either perspective.

These days, you can also learn a lot from business books, some of which might take you months to read and absorb. And they may have something to offer small business owners, managers, or anyone interested in learning about business.

Built, Not Born, however, is a short book that is long on common sense, facts, advice, and business wisdom. Wisdom that comes from over five decades of starting new businesses, running a highly successful national corporation, mentoring entrepreneurs of all ages, and investing millions of dollars in small business enterprises. You can read this book in the time it takes to fly from New York to San Francisco. I've cut out anything extraneous and focused on what I feel all entrepreneurs and entrepreneurial employees must know to succeed, backed by real-life, been-there-done-that experiences.

This book is targeted at those of you who are considering starting or buying a business, or those who are running a thriving business—or a struggling one. It is also written for entrepreneurial employees who want to run their department or division more effectively and more profitably.

PREFACE

From my one-page business plan to why employment may be riskier than entrepreneurship, from the importance of a prenuptial or postnuptial agreement to the power of a pregnant pause, you will discover the secrets of how I grew a business from a few thousand dollars to a multibillion-dollar enterprise with more than half a million customers. My aim is to help you become more successful and hopefully entertain you along the way.

It's your choice: you can spend the next few years working toward a master of business administration, or you can start your business life right now. In only a few hours, you will gain a thorough understanding of how to succeed in business. Thank you for picking up this book. Turn the page and learn the not-so-secret secrets to success.

INTRODUCTION

If you've spent your hard-earned money to purchase this book, I think you deserve to know a little about the person who wrote it and how he came by all the business wisdom and advice it contains. Unlike many books on the market, none of what I'll tell you in these pages is theory. I'm going to share with you what I learned when, with $3,000 and a credit card, I took a basic business idea and turned it into one of America's largest and most profitable corporations.

My goal is to help you do things the right way—the first time. When you review the table of contents of this book, I hope you say to yourself, "This stuff is important to me and my business." In *Built, Not Born* you won't find buzzwords, wild promises, unnecessary information, or hyperbole. What you *will* find is solid business advice that, if taken, will make your life easier and help you become more successful. I'll also tell you the stories behind how some of my key business beliefs took shape and describe the circumstances that led to my adopting them as my own successful business strategies.

The biggest challenge facing entrepreneurs is that most don't have the benefit of over fifty years' experience mastering their trade, fifty years of making mistakes and finding ways not only to correct them but also to ensure they don't make them again. They haven't fought their way through seemingly impossible challenges and dealt with idiots, phonies, and others who seem to delight in hampering their progress. It's this experience that I bring to the businesses I invest in, and now to those of you who read this book.

In today's ever-changing business world, where augmented reality (AR) is actually a thing, and there is an Internet of Things (IoT), I sought an old-school way of allowing you to invite me into your business: through the pages of this book. And incidentally, this book will never crash on you—no blue screen of death, I promise. Just keep turning the pages and I'll be with you every step of the way. Of course, that's not to say you won't also hear me on a podcast in the very near future.

My advice will sometimes fly in the face of perceived business wisdom; in fact, it will often question standard practices and defy the status quo. Throughout my life I've challenged the ways things are done in business, sports, politics, and philanthropy. Why? To increase my chances of winning in business and life while still offering a good deal for everyone. In this book, for the first time I'll share my no-nonsense, sometimes contrarian, principles and business approaches with you: the ones that turned the son of Sicilian immigrants from West Irondequoit, New York, into a multibillionaire.

Built, Not Born will give you an edge. It will tell you how to turn the odds of success in your favor, improve productivity and profitability, reduce risks, and avoid the many pitfalls lying in wait for unwary and inexperienced businesspeople.

Where It All Started

When I launched a small payroll processing company back in 1971, I had no idea it would become the corporate giant and industry leader that Paychex is today. All I wanted to do was make enough money to support my family and ensure that my developmentally disabled son would never have to live in a state-run facility.

The concept for Paychex originated when I was a salesman in the payroll processing sector for EAS (Electronic Accounting Systems), a competitor of the industry leader, ADP (Automatic Data Processing). Like every other payroll processing company, EAS targeted companies with fifty or more employees. At the time, it was an industry-wide belief that outside payroll services were viable only for large companies.

No one had ever thought to challenge that principle, and I love a good challenge, especially if it tests commonly held beliefs that don't stand up to scrutiny. I started to question the reasoning behind why small businesses with fewer than fifty employees wouldn't need our services even more than larger companies did.

I went to the library—that was how long ago this was, pre-internet—and discovered that approximately 95 percent of businesses in America had fifty employees or fewer. That was a *huge* market the company I worked for was ignoring. On my own time, I spent several months talking to small businesses and accountants and testing my financial assumptions. More importantly, I figured out a way to deliver payroll services to this market at a price these small businesses could afford.

Once I had proven to myself there was indeed a market the industry leaders were missing, I talked to my bosses at EAS. I presented my findings, expecting that they would support me in approaching this promising new market. Unfortunately, as much as I tried to sell them on my business concept, they didn't share my level of excitement or optimism. No matter what I said, my bosses refused to believe the under-fifty-employee businesses were a worthwhile market. Their reasons included: "They can't afford to outsource payroll," "The profit would be too low," and "Their accountants won't like it." Doggedly, I challenged their assumptions, but I was constantly faced with negative responses.

So, like many entrepreneurs before me, I decided to go it alone. I took what little money I had ($3,000) and the industry knowledge I had gained while working at EAS and launched Paymaster—a company now known as Paychex, which has a market value of $28 billion. In case you're wondering about that figure, a company's market value is calculated by multiplying its outstanding shares by its current market price.

Defying the status quo is what entrepreneurs do every day. I had spotted an opportunity, challenged an industry norm, and targeted all the "little guys"—entrepreneurs who weren't worth the effort to other companies.

To many people, payroll processing doesn't sound glamorous. On the face of it, it's hard to be passionate about the payroll industry. But success doesn't always depend on *what* you sell—it's about the business itself. I was excited about the opportunity to build a solid business and earn good money. I recognized that small businesses and the entrepreneurs who ran them had nowhere to go if they wanted help with their payroll, except perhaps their local CPAs—and those people didn't even like doing payroll. My passion came from providing a much-needed service to a very large, untapped market.

As a result, I uncovered and opened up a market so big that Paychex and its competitors have mined perhaps only 20 percent of its potential. Even though ADP had a twenty-five-year head start, Paychex is closing in on the market leader. Currently, Paychex provides payroll and human resources (HR) services to several hundred thousand clients and employs over fifteen thousand people. Who said there wasn't a market?

Why Did I Write This Book?

Not long ago I was speaking at a conference, and during the Q&A period a woman asked me, "How many people have you had to trample on to get to where you are today?" My answer was, "None. I decided long ago that it was far better and more effective to bring people along with me."

The question she asked is not an uncommon one. People look at me and see a multibillionaire businessman, so of course they believe I had to be ruthless—or unscrupulous at the very least. And when people look at a successful company like Paychex, many are tempted to think the successful businessperson behind it has an aggressive, step-on-people-and-claw-your-way-to-the-top-at-any-cost attitude, perhaps inherited money, or maybe experienced a healthy measure of luck. In my case, none of this was true. The first few years were tough, very tough, but I always focused on bringing people along with me rather than using them or taking advantage of them.

That said, I know of many businesspeople (and many more politicians) who have clawed their way to the top by being less than fair, taking little notice of the collateral damage they leave in their wake.

However, my answer to that woman was incomplete. Sure, I have always attempted to bring people along with me and to be fair and aboveboard with everyone I deal with, but I don't believe that alone has helped me become the businessman I am today or has been entirely responsible for the success I have enjoyed. She made me think about my accomplishments and ask myself, What *has* been my approach or strategy? Is there something definable that contributed to my success? Did I have something I could share that would help America's thirty million small business owners[1] become more successful?

If so, what was it? Was there a magic bullet, or was it just luck? I'm not alone in thinking that luck in business is a myth. To adapt a well-worn quote, "Luck is when hard work meets opportunity." But even that is too simplistic. A better answer is that I learned (sometimes the hard way) how businesses work, how they function on a day-to-day basis. I looked at how small businesses operated, and I studied their interior workings, the arithmetic, the relationships, and the mistakes people make. I questioned *everything*.

I'm never satisfied with the way things are just because they've always been that way. The fact is, I see things a little, or maybe a lot, differently than other people, particularly other businesspeople.

I made a business (and a good life) out of helping small businesses and entrepreneurs run their companies more effectively. With my customers I always felt that *their business was my business*. In this book I share everything I did to make it to where I am today. I share the things you can start doing today to turn your ideas and concepts into profitable, competitive, and thriving businesses where you can be in charge of your own destiny.

Beyond Business

I discovered a long time ago that the lessons I've learned in business are applicable to other parts of my life. I found these principles useful during my political career, in my foray into owning a sports team, and even in my philanthropic endeavors.

Although in the corporate world I am best known for being the founder and current chairman of Paychex, I've been challenging the status quo for a long time—and not only in the business world.

In 1991, I cofounded a political party called the Independence Party, and I ran three times for governor of New York.

I bought the bankrupt and losing Buffalo Sabres hockey team in 2003 and turned around the franchise, both in terms of financial health and by transforming them into a winning team. I had watched the team play only three times before I bought it, and I wasn't a huge hockey fan. But just as I did in business, I questioned everything about the way the team was managed, including entrenched strategies. I treated hockey as a business, not a hobby, which was an innovative and somewhat foreign approach to many franchise owners back then. It wasn't long, however, before they sat up and took notice.

In terms of playing well, things really started going right for us in the 2005–06 season. We had one of the best lineups in the league, and we began to dominate the competition—we were faster and better than anyone else. We reached the conference finals of the Stanley Cup that year and again in 2006–07, posting consecutive fifty-win seasons. In that same season, for the first time in Sabres history, we won the Presidents' Trophy. To add to our glory, we were among just five teams to make consecutive appearances in the conference finals since the lockout in 2004.

In 2006, I was personally asked by former president Bill Clinton to be the founding sponsor and underwriter of the Clinton Global Initiative (CGI). In that capacity I was honored to work closely with kings and queens, presidents, and high-profile activist celebrities. This was not a case of purely handing over a check and getting name recognition; I treated this global nonprofit enterprise just like a business. People are amazed (at the time some of his staff were horrified) when they hear that I sat President Clinton down and insisted we go over one of the CGI conference budgets line by line together.

Today, I split my time between working with the young businesses I've invested in since retiring from Paychex and running my family's charitable foundation. Over the past twenty years I have donated more than $250 million to worthy causes. If you follow the principles and strategies outlined in this book you, too, may be able to spread the benefits of your success well beyond yourself and your shareholders.

I've been the primary funder of eight medical institutions, including three Golisano Children's Hospitals, which have helped tens of thousands of patients regain their health and have saved many lives. I also established the first-ever global Leadership Award for Exemplary Health Care Services. And my global health work with Special Olympics (training medical professionals to treat Special Olympic athletes) led to me being recognized as one of *Forbes* magazine's "Philanthropy's Big Bets for Social Change of 2015."

I am passionate about education, and I have worked with the Rochester Institute of Technology to make possible the Thomas Golisano College of Computing and Information Sciences and the Golisano Institute for Sustainability. In addition, I have been happy to support the efforts of many other colleges and schools, including St. John Fisher College, Niagara University, Roberts Wesleyan College, Ave Maria University, Nazareth College, Hartwick College of Oneonta, and Bishop Kearney High School.

As previously mentioned, today Paychex is worth $28 billion. It has more than 670,000 customers and more than 15,500 employees working out of more than 100 locations across the United States and northern Europe. In fact, one in every twelve private-sector employees in America receives their paycheck from Paychex. Although I retired fifteen years ago, I remain chairman of the board.

A Personal Note

This is the book I wish I'd had when I was a young father with a wife at home and a son with serious medical needs, and I decided to start my own company. It wasn't easy. But I'd do it again in a heartbeat. This book is dedicated to entrepreneurs everywhere, for whom I have nothing but respect, admiration, and affection. They are the backbone of the US economy. Be brave, be fair, act with integrity, and above all, always try to create a good deal for everyone.

ONE

ENTREPRENEURSHIP:

A Risk Worth Taking

Not everyone can—or should—be an entrepreneur, but not because of the risks involved. Let me be clear: nothing in life is without risk. Relying on a job can be one of the riskiest things you do. In this chapter we'll explore entrepreneurship; the risks, rewards, and challenges; what you can do to start becoming a better businessperson; and why it's the most exciting "job" in the world.

The Risk Explored

If you are running your own company or trying to grow your business, you already know it can be an unpredictable and stressful way of life. If you're considering starting out on your own, are you having nightmares about the potential risk? Are other people telling you not to do it? Do your parents, spouse, and friends think you're crazy? I can empathize. I had an accountant tell me I wouldn't make it. I even had business leaders tell me my plan for their industry was unworkable. But here I am, almost fifty years later, and the company I launched back in 1971 continues to grow every day, every month, every year. The thing is, you can manage risk.

Being Employed Is Not Risk-Free

Those people who talk about the risks involved in starting and growing a business seem to imply that having a job is risk-free—get a job, be set for life. Was that ever true? In reality, working for a company is not as risk-free as it might have been a generation or two ago. Cradle-to-grave jobs have gone the way of pay phones and Blockbuster Video stores. During the second half of the twentieth century, people focused on job security by working for large companies. Those kinds of jobs don't exist anymore.

There's an excellent example right here where I live in Rochester, New York. In 1982, Eastman Kodak had about sixty thousand employees; today it has fewer than ten thousand. Nobody knows with certainty where the next disruption is coming from. Couple this with amazing advances in technology, and there is a case to be made that being *employed* is the risky alternative.

Moreover, if you are fortunate enough to have a good job with a good company, you are always at the whim of a bad boss. Even if that's not the case, your division could be performing well, but the company itself might enter a period of financial difficulty. There's a lot of insecurity working for other people; don't let anyone tell you differently.

One other thing: you can't sell a job or pass it along to your heirs. Build a successful business, however, and it can provide income and security in retirement; not only that, it can outlive you.

Let me delve a little deeper into this whole risk thing. I admit, there's always risk in business, sometimes significant risk, but that's true of everything in life. When I first started the publication *Bidders Guide*, which I will tell you about later, I had a young family, and it was a risk. It was an even bigger risk when I left a good (but not great) paying job to launch Paymaster, and I certainly felt nervous about making the leap. But I'd thought it through, done my research, and determined it was a calculated risk.

If you feel starting your own business might be for you and you have a good idea, don't be a wimp. Seriously, the dangers of owning a business can be minimized. The first thing you need is a complete understanding of how the business world operates, how companies work, what your responsibilities are when you head up a company, and finally what strategies work and which ones to avoid. That's what this book provides, so read on.

Do You Question Every Business You See? If Not, You Need to Start

What makes a good entrepreneur? Are they born or made? Some people can't stop themselves from thinking in terms of business opportunities. For instance, if you've ever sat next to a food truck, eating your hamburger, and counted the number of patrons purchasing food and then multiplied this by the average amount spent and then extrapolated what the business owner would earn in a typical lunch period, you're probably an entrepreneur. If you then went further and estimated the food truck's operating costs and calculated its net profit, you are definitely an entrepreneur—even if you don't realize it.

If, on the other hand, during your lunch break at a taco stand you ate your taco while dreaming of what it would be like to own a food truck because, heck, you love tacos, everyone likes tacos, so you think you could make a huge success out of it, you might want to reconsider starting your own business.

I was in Cuba recently on vacation and visited a cigar factory (I'm known for my love of a good cigar), and my first instinct was to ask questions: Where did they source their materials? What was their output? How many workers did they have and what did those workers get paid? I got a lot of pleasure figuring out the economics of that cigar factory, its profitability and sustainability. Whether it's a local toy store, a restaurant, or any other business, the entrepreneur in me wants to see which businesses are winning, which are losing, and more importantly, why.

Natural entrepreneurs are curious. They constantly question and challenge business scenarios. They are always looking for an angle, a way to make things work better or introduce a new product or service. They are always thinking and planning.

I've always been entrepreneurial, not out of some genetic predisposition toward selling anything in particular but more out of a desire to have enough money to meet my lifestyle needs and those of my family, and to be independent.

When I was a kid my parents didn't have money to spare, so I never got an allowance. If I wanted money to spend, I had to discover a way to go out and earn it. When I was about ten, I hauled a little red wagon around our neighborhood with a friend, collecting old newspapers. Once we had filled the wagon, my father would take us to the dump, where we'd get paid a few pennies for our efforts. It wasn't much, but I liked the feeling of those coins in my pocket—they felt a lot like independence. That same wagon did double duty when, sometime later, I got a paper route delivering the Rochester *Democrat and Chronicle*.

When I was fifteen, I often hung out with a friend, Dick Chesler, at the local bowling alley. Bowling was big in those days, and the local North Park Lanes was humming every weekend. If all the lanes were busy, patrons had to take a ticket with a number and wait their turn to pay for a lane when one became available. Our active, make-a-buck-any-way-we-can minds realized we could offer a service to anyone willing to pay a few dollars to get a lane sooner. Just ahead of busy periods we would arrive and surreptitiously take a number of tickets. When the number on one of our tickets was close to being called, we'd offer it to new arrivals who were facing a long wait for a lane—for a price of course. Eventually the manager noticed what we were doing and threw us out, but for a while it was a profitable small-business enterprise. Even back then I saw the value of identifying a need and the benefit of offering everyone a good deal, while making a little money for myself.

Over one busy Christmas period I worked for the US Postal Service. That's where I learned what it was like to have an eight-to-five government job. I was given a route that was supposed to take eight hours. When I finished by noon on my first day, I expected my manager to be impressed, but instead he was insistent that the route should take eight hours and that I must have missed some houses. I assured him I hadn't. He in turn, with a serious, almost threatening stare, made sure I understood that he did not expect to see me back before five. From that point on, I spent my afternoons hanging out with a friend. That was my first and last federal government job—getting full-time pay for half-time work. It's no wonder to this day I have little confidence in the government's ability to manage anything efficiently and cost effectively.

Why Do You Want to Become an Entrepreneur and Should You?

Not everyone comes to entrepreneurship naturally. For some it is less about being fascinated with the way businesses operate and more about a desire to bring a product or service to market. For others it can be born out of necessity due to being laid off from a job or being stuck in a boring, dead-end career. Increasingly, seniors are turning to entrepreneurship as a way to supplement their retirement income.

Still others have entrepreneurship thrust on them, which reminds me of my early days in Paychex when I invited personal and business friends to join me in the venture. Looking back at my seventeen partners and franchisees, none of them were what I would call natural entrepreneurs. It was interesting to watch how some adapted well to the cut and thrust of business and others lacked initiative and self-motivation.

This disparity would prove challenging when I decided we needed to go through a consolidation process and incorporate into a single business, whereby partners and franchisees all became shareholders. I had some people who had opened several new branches and others who had not expanded at all. The latter seemed to enjoy the fruits of our success a little too much and were more concerned with their golf handicap than with growing the business. These varying levels of ambition were taken into consideration when shares were allocated, much to the chagrin of some of my colleagues. More about that later.

Take a Chance or Sit on the Sidelines

I offered my best friend, Gene Polisseni, a chance to become my business partner in Paychex right from the outset, but he turned it down. He was running a tire store in Rochester at the time, and he couldn't see the potential of a payroll processing business. He is a case of someone who simply didn't have the entrepreneurial gene (pun intended).

As Paychex expanded and the number of partners and franchises grew, there he was, my best friend, watching it all from the sidelines. I was running out of decent territories and partnership opportunities, so I attempted one last time to bring him on board. I called him and said, "Okay, Gene, here's the deal. I want to come over to your house on Sunday evening and I want you and Wanda [his wife] to listen to my pitch. Make sure the kids are out of the house—I want your undivided attention. Can we do this?"

He agreed, and that Sunday I laid out the opportunity as clearly as I could—the company dynamics, the financials, the salesmanship, the product, everything. I told them they should move to Cincinnati, Ohio, because it was the best market I had left, a territory that included Louisville and Dayton.

The presentation took me a full three hours—I was serious. I knew it would be an uphill battle as Gene loved Rochester and was very active in the community, not to mention he had four children and Wanda to consider. It took them a few days to mull it over, but he called me and said, "Yeah, we're going to move." That was in 1977; financially he did well, but if he'd been less risk-averse and joined me when I first asked him in 1971, he would have become far wealthier.

You have to assess a business opportunity for what it is. You don't have to love the product or service; you just have to recognize the potential.

Are You Cut Out for the Lifestyle?

Being an entrepreneur is hugely rewarding, but make no mistake, it's hard work and there will be times when you'll be backed up against a wall and you'll feel like giving up. Don't.

I remember being close to giving up once, in the early days of Paychex. It was a Fourth of July weekend, and we'd developed new software so that we could run our own payrolls instead of relying on my old employer, EAS, to process them. I'd been assured the software would be ready for the long weekend, but when the time came, it wouldn't print checks. To put this into perspective, if we couldn't deliver payrolls, workers would not get paid and our credibility would be destroyed; everything we had worked for would be lost.

I'd already canceled my arrangement with EAS, so I had to go back to them and ask for assistance. Thankfully they sent a couple of technicians over to our offices to help us out. I think the senior management at EAS may have believed our dream of striking out on our own was just that, a dream, and that we'd be back using their services the following week. Of course, that never happened. We all worked through the night and managed to complete the payrolls, but it was too late to mail them, so we had another major problem. We had to call in any and all friends to help, and we got the payrolls to our clients any way we could, by car, motorcycle, whatever we could think of at the time.

I remember that period well; it was hectic and stressful. I lost something like ten pounds and didn't manage to get home for seven days. I looked a mess. I'd been sleeping on the floor of my office. I was toast—burned toast. But when I walked in the door, my then-wife, Gloria, took a long look at me and said, "You can't quit. Just keep putting one foot after another."

It was good advice. We stuck with the plan, took one day at a time, and survived the crisis. I'd like to say that was the only major crisis during my thirty-plus years as CEO of Paychex, but I'd be lying. Running a business, any business, means challenges, some expected and others that come out of the blue. It comes with the territory. It's an old aphorism, but it's true nevertheless: if you can't stand the heat, get out of the kitchen.

Talking about kitchens, as I mentioned earlier, several years before I founded Paychex, I started a business publication called *Bidders Guide*. I gathered all the advertisements calling for bids on public contracts from local newspapers and then sorted them by product category and placed them in the guide, which was published three times a week. The publication was sold on subscription to companies that wanted to ensure they didn't miss any selling opportunities.

I was married with two children at the time, and we were struggling financially. I remember Gene came to visit one day. He walked into the kitchen and opened the fridge, and when he saw it was empty, he took us all out for dinner. He was a good friend, and to this day I wish he had been with me from the beginning of my Paychex adventure. Maybe that day he found our cupboards bare was in part to blame for why he was reticent about leaving his job at the tire store and joining me at Paychex. He'd witnessed how tough setting out on your own can be.

I sold *Bidders Guide* a short time later, and the $3,000 I netted was the seed money I used to start Paychex. Recently I ran into the new owners of the guide and am pleased to report that after fifty years, it's still going strong.

Becoming a Better Entrepreneur

Regardless of how you became a businessperson, or where you are today in business, you can improve your business skills and become a better entrepreneur. I often meet people who for one reason or another have a business idea and want to launch a new enterprise, but they are not there yet in terms of business acumen. Maybe that's you. Perhaps on an entrepreneurial scale of one to ten you consider yourself a five. That's good; being honest with yourself is the first step to success.

To become a ten, you need to understand what makes businesses successful; you need to know what you need to know. You need to be intimately knowledgeable about your industry. Being successful as an entrepreneur requires comprehensive knowledge of the workings of your business, your product or service, your market, and your industry. Sure, you can employ others to do the stuff you may not be skilled at or enjoy doing, but that doesn't mean you don't need to fully understand every aspect of your business.

The Rewards of an Entrepreneurial Life

My childhood entrepreneurial activities aside, there are many reasons I became a lifelong entrepreneur. The most important was the potential of unlimited earnings and personal and economic independence. I also valued the freedom to choose the people I wanted to work with and those I didn't.

In my opinion, the benefits far outweigh the drawbacks. Ask yourself if you like the idea of being your own boss, setting your own course, creating something new. Are independence and freedom important to you? Do you put a high level of importance on creating something that may well outlive you? Would you like the satisfaction of knowing you are contributing to the economy, providing employment for a great number of people, and meeting the needs of so many customers? I always have.

You can choose whatever industry you want and whatever product or service you want to sell, with one caveat: you need to know an enormous amount about your industry and what you are selling.

Finally, entrepreneurship offers you the potential of unlimited earnings and the ability to create the lifestyle you desire for yourself and for your family. In the end it's about having ultimate control over your life.

How Do I Spot a Good Entrepreneur?

Too many wannabe entrepreneurs have no idea what running a business entails; even worse, they have little to no idea how to assess whether their business concept has a chance of getting off the ground. People come to me all the time with business ideas, looking for investment and mentorship, but the vast majority don't get past the two guys I have who screen the business proposals I receive. A good, or even great, concept is not enough.

Personally, I look for two things when considering whether a business has a chance of success. First, I want to see that the business owner has worked in the industry. They have to possess intimate knowledge of their market, their product or service, and their customers—they have to be familiar with the environment. Second, an entrepreneur needs to possess a sense of reality. Too often passion overtakes common sense. Too often entrepreneurs have an inflated opinion as to what percentage of the market they can realistically expect in the first few years. I'll deal with this topic in more detail in chapter 7, "Lead, Follow, or Get Out of the Way."

I also assess a person's attitude. I can help them become a better entrepreneur or businessperson, but I have to see passion, commitment, and a little humility—a willingness to learn.

Entrepreneurial Employees

Not all entrepreneurs run their own businesses; some are entrepreneurial employees. These are people who don't just do their job to a level that satisfies their bosses but take it upon themselves to make the company as successful as possible—in a sense they take ownership.

When I was running Paychex, these were the people I sought out and encouraged to come and work for me. I've met this special breed of person when buying anything from tires and cars to computers; they are entrepreneurial by nature. Some ended up working for Paychex, and others came to me later with business ideas in which I invested. I helped them make the transition from working for someone else to working for themselves. I have always found these types of people worth investing in; they give me a good return not only on my financial investment but also on the time I spend mentoring them.

—————— Takeaways ——————

- Entrepreneurship is not as risky as you might think.
- Being employed is not risk-free.
- Entrepreneurs constantly question and challenge business scenarios and always look for a way to make things work better or introduce a new product or service.
- Take a chance or sit on the sidelines; it's your choice.
- Ask yourself why you want to be an entrepreneur. Are you cut out for the lifestyle?
- Entrepreneurship can be taught and learned. Consider how much you know about running a business and identify what further education you need.
- Perseverance is a valuable entrepreneurial trait.
- Entrepreneurs should possess an intimate knowledge of their market, the product or service, and their customers— they have to be familiar with the environment.
- Be realistic when assessing the market share your business

might achieve, especially when approaching investors. Entrepreneurs are optimists, but they also need a sense of reality.

- Entrepreneurship offers the potential of unlimited earnings and the ability to create the lifestyle you desire for yourself and for your family. In the end it's about having ultimate control over your life.
- Not all entrepreneurs run their own businesses. Are you, or could you be, an entrepreneurial employee?

TWO

UNDERSTAND YOUR BUSINESS

Viability on One Page

The basics of running a business haven't changed since trade began. Sure, we have the internet and social media, and digital technology is advancing faster than many of us can keep up with, but when it comes down to it, the most important part of a business boils down to a few simple calculations on a single page. I'm talking about a profit and loss projection that shows you immediately what you have to do to turn a profit.

Tell me about any business opportunity, and I can grab a piece of paper and outline a plan detailing how it might become profitable—on a single page. My initial business plan for Paychex was exactly that: one page. I calculated what my operating costs were and discovered how many clients I needed to sell to break even. In many ways it's that simple. If I'm a retailer selling popcorn, how many people do I need to come through the door and buy my popcorn to allow me to pay all my bills and give myself an income? The rest is strategy, useful but peripheral.

Recently I was sitting in my car outside a video game store. It wasn't in a good location, and I watched how few people were going into the store and even fewer coming out with a purchase. The arithmetic wasn't complicated: the average price of a game is not very high, and the sheer numbers required to pay for overhead (rent, utilities, inventory, etc.), let alone an income for the owner, meant there would have to be a continuous stream of people entering the store for the business to be profitable. Let's look at the basic math:

ANNUAL OVERHEAD ON A SMALL STORE

Rent	$15,000
Utilities	$3,600
Employee	$20,000
Freight	$1,000
Professional fees	$5,000
Owner's salary	$60,000
Misc.	$6,000
Total	*$110,600*

If we take the average price of a sale as $60 with a gross margin of 40 percent, this results in a gross profit of $24 per sale.

This is where it gets interesting. If we divide the store's overhead (bear in mind we are using the barest minimum of expenses) by the gross profit made on each sale, we can see that the store needs to make 4,608 sales per year. If the store were open 6 days a week for 52 weeks per year, which is 312 days a year, they would need almost 15 sales a day, every day. Of course, sales at Christmas would be more vigorous and the sale of used games delivers a higher profit margin, but the need to have a consistent flow of customers purchasing something every day makes it very doubtful the business could be successful at this location.

I have used this quick-and-easy, one-page calculation countless times to quickly ascertain the viability of a business concept, and after I have done a full financial workup on the business, it is usually proven correct.

Business Planning

I'm not a fan of business plans that could double as doorstops. Who's going to read a thirty-thousand-word plan? Actually, I'm not a fan of the business plan document itself, although I do believe entrepreneurs have to thoroughly understand everything to do with their business. My advice is to focus on the key points and financials that demonstrate your business concept is viable and cut the rest of the verbiage. The peripheral stats, five- and ten-year projections, and other useless elements of many business plans can be ditched; they're not fooling anyone. These "by the pound" business plans are often used in an attempt to justify the author's claims. They are crammed with documents containing masses of statistical information and projections, or as I like to call it, "fluff." Business plans should keep to the basics.

The second piece of advice I'm going to give you is to keep it real. Nothing turns off a lender or an investor more than exaggerated or poorly thought-out statements, promises, and projections.

People come to me all the time with what they consider a great idea with nothing to back up their claim. These people start and close businesses every day. There is no sense of reality to what they are trying to achieve. In retail, for instance, location and the type of product they are trying to sell can make it impossible to make enough money to survive—but people keep trying.

To me, it's a simple calculation, as you saw with my simple analysis above, but very few people do the math. They let passion cloud their judgment. That's the myth many business books peddle: "Follow your passion," or "Believe it and you'll achieve it." That sort of thinking can lead you down a dangerous path.

The most important thing when planning your business should be the accuracy of your facts and statistics. You need to be able to provide proof of the veracity of your figures. If I see a plan that states a business is going to capture 10 percent of the market, I'm suspicious; warning bells are ringing. Today, in spite of decades of history in the market, if you combine ADP, Paychex, and Intuit (the third-largest player in payroll processing) together, they still only have less than 20 percent of the potential payroll processing market. Wildly inflated projections are common. Sometimes they can simply be the result of overenthusiasm on the part of the entrepreneur, but they can also be used to mislead the reader. Understanding your market, or the market someone is trying to get you to invest in, is of paramount importance. The same is true when buying a business, but I'll talk more about that later.

A few years ago, someone came to me with a new HR product for employers. He was hoping to sell it to Paychex's customers with one thousand employees or more, which he excitedly stated was 10 percent of our company's clients. He estimated that number to be fifty thousand clients, then he multiplied that figure by one thousand to come up with the market for his product of fifty million employees. That's all good; in fact, it sounds great, doesn't it?

Guess what? Paychex delivered only twelve million W-2s the previous year. The market could never be fifty million people. It's easy to get the math wrong, especially if you haven't done enough research and don't have knowledge and understanding of the market and industry in which you are operating.

All too often entrepreneurs get carried away with their sales forecasts and try to make the statistics tell the story they want to hear themselves and to promote to others. In the case above, the reality is the average Paychex customer doesn't have one thousand employees; it has sixteen—and that's a massive difference. Projections mean nothing if the person creating them doesn't fully understand the market.

The myth of business plans is that they are used in an attempt to sell the reader on the strength of a business concept, either to encourage investment or convince a lender to commit funds. In many cases, the numbers are inflated and unrealistic at best and duplicitous at worst. Don't forget, at some point someone is going to compare your projections to your results. I repeat, projections don't mean anything if you haven't done your homework.

Another important thing not only to understand but to accept with every fiber of your being is that a first-rate business plan can often tell you *not* to start the business at all but run away and run fast. It's critical that you take a hard look at the actual numbers and be candid with yourself about what they are telling you.

As I said earlier, I'm not a proponent of the business plan document, but I do believe that every entrepreneur should plan their business. And during the planning stages they need to be brutally honest with themselves and with those from whom they are asking financial assistance.

Whether you decide to formalize your research into an actual document or not is up to you, but what follows is an overview of the key questions you need to answer and the information you need to gather.

A good start might be to create a mission statement. Paychex's first mission statement was "Sell clients, service clients, and make money." Sometimes it's as simple as that.

Before I take you through what I consider to be the must-have knowledge when planning your business, I'll tell you the three most important things investors and lenders need to see before deciding whether they are interested in supporting your business.

1. Executive Summary

This is a one- or two-page summary of your business concept, the industry, your market, and the highlights of how your business will operate. This is a quick overview, so investors can put into perspective what you are about to tell them.

2. Profit and Loss Statement

Sometimes referred to as an income statement, this is the one-page assessment I mentioned earlier. Educated readers will immediately be able to tell from this document and the executive summary whether you have a grasp of the fundamentals of your business. At this point they will either carry on reading or throw your pitch in the trash. Trust me, I trash more than I read.

3. Human Resources (Personnel)

If you still have their attention at this point, you have an opportunity to show them that both you and your management team have enough industry, market, and product knowledge to know what the heck you are doing. In chapter 7, "Lead, Follow, or Get Out of the Way," I'll discuss this point in more detail; for now, trust me, you cannot fake this.

The rest of your business planning is important, but without the sections outlined above, it doesn't mean a whole lot, as you may never get people to listen to the rest of what you have to say. What follows is not a tutorial on writing a business plan; it is a guide to what someone like me who invests millions of dollars annually in start-ups and early-stage businesses expects a business owner to know about their business. I don't care if it's written down; it's stuff you need to know so you have all the answers when an investor or lender comes to you with questions.

I'll be talking about these areas in the chapters that follow, but first, take a look at the type of information you need to gather and know before you start your business venture.

Product or Service

What are you selling and why? Why have you decided this product or service will add to what is already being offered by other companies? Why should people or businesses buy what you are selling?

I remember identifying the need for the *Bidders Guide* during my time selling business machines at the Burroughs Corporation. I was on a sales call at the administrative offices of a village in upstate New York, and the town clerk was interested in buying an accounting machine to do water billing. I'd made several presentations and followed all their processes. The town clerk liked the machine and seemed to like me, so things were looking good. Back at the office I told my branch manager I was close to a sale and he asked me, "Where are they going to put their bid advertisement?"

At first I was confused, but I quickly learned that in most states, when a purchase exceeded a certain dollar amount, school districts and municipalities were required to advertise openly for bids. In part, this was to send a message to the public that their tax dollars were being spent wisely.

My manager at Burroughs said, "Get them to advertise in the local newspaper where no one will see it." It took me a minute, but then I realized this strategy was intended to lessen the odds of our competition seeing the bid advertisement. My immediate thought was, *How many times do our competitors do the same thing to us?* My second thought was, *How much would businesses be prepared to pay to access all procurement notices in one place at one time, rather than buying every newspaper in the state or risk missing valuable opportunities?*

Identifying and being able to demonstrate a strong need for what you sell is integral to a good business plan.

Financials

A business's financials are more telling, prophetic if you like, than any other facts, statements, or information you provide, so you need to take them seriously. In a formal business plan, they're usually pushed to the back. That makes no sense to me; they should be up front and given the respect they deserve.

If you can't read and understand financial statements, one of your first jobs is to educate yourself. I'll give you a primer in the next chapter to get you started. If you are already familiar with and can read these documents, good for you. Now start improving your overall understanding of financial statements.

Industry and Market Sector

In what industry will, or does, your business operate? How does your business fit within that industry? Don't fall into the trap of trying to tell the history of the industry or include peripheral facts and statistics. Keep your comments specific to your particular position in the industry today, the sector you fall into, and the size of the market sector in which you will operate.

Customers

Who are they? Where are they? Where do they currently buy similar products or services to yours? What is their socioeconomic status? Why will they buy what you sell? What is the size of the market and how much of it are you likely to capture? Show you understand the financial limitations of your typical customers and how you will target them more effectively.

Market Research

Too many entrepreneurs try to guess the characteristics of their market instead of doing the prerequisite market research. These days market research is easy; you have the internet. When I launched *Bidders Guide* all I had was the local library. Before deciding to launch the publication, I spent many hours learning everything I could about government procurement along with the companies that answered bid notices—the companies that would become my customers.

Do not try to guess the characteristics of your market; go out and discover them. Along the way you will find surprises, identify new markets, and uncover additional products and services that your market requires.

Market research is the cornerstone of business planning. Everything hinges on the information you gather. Market research gives your plan credibility. It also will give you peace of mind. Without market research your business planning is fiction or, worse, fantasy!

Competition

I'll talk more about this later, but know one thing: every business has competition, either direct or indirect; your job is to carve out a piece of the pie for your company. Your plan should provide a realistic assessment of your competition and your strategy for getting a share of the market.

Price

Too often entrepreneurs overestimate what customers are willing to pay for what they sell. The research you do on your competition will help you come up with a price that people are used to paying and that will also provide your company with the profit it requires to be successful.

Marketing

Every business requires a unique promotional strategy. The market research you carry out, especially on your prospective customers, will help you identify where you need to advertise. In today's social media–crazy world, the options are almost endless, but when developing your marketing strategy and budget, keep it real.

Sales

A business plan needs to show the reader how the business will sell its products and services. Your marketing strategy will demonstrate how you will get what you sell noticed, but you also need to prove you have a strategy to bring in orders. Outline in your sales process how you will identify prospects, qualify them, contact them, and then sell to them.

Sitting by the telephone waiting for it to ring is not a sales strategy.

Production

If you are going to manufacture something, you will need to demonstrate the process you go through to end up with the finished product. Include information on the equipment required, the cost, the production facility, output capacity, inventory requirements, and access to raw materials and suppliers.

Distribution

How are you going to get your product to your customer? Will you deliver it yourself? Employ a delivery person? Get sales staff to deliver it when taking orders? Mail it? Courier it? And, of course, what will it cost?

Administration

What legal business structure are you proposing? Proprietorship, a partnership, a corporation? Before deciding which legal structure is best, get advice from your accountant and lawyer. Before that, however, read the section below to get an overview of your options.

Business Structures—I'm Not Talking Buildings

Although the process of legally forming a company has become easier over the years, especially with online legal services and standardized documents, the decision as to which legal structure you should choose is still complex, a decision made more complicated because of annual changes to tax regulations.

At some point, however, you are going to have to decide how to legally structure your business. Much will depend on how you plan to operate now and how you see things developing in the future. I suggest you build in as much flexibility as you can from the outset, as things have a habit of changing rapidly. The two most important things to consider initially are liability and taxation.

You may think that flexibility is not an issue, that you know how your business is going to grow and what it will look like in several years' time, but things change. When I first started Paychex, I was focused solely on the Rochester area and had no plans to service a larger territory, let alone the whole of the country, but I ended up bringing partners on board and selling franchises. Later we consolidated into one large corporation and eventually went public.

The legal structure of the business had to change many times over the years, and every time it did, the legal and accounting fees were not insignificant. Had I thought about, or even considered, potential growth, I would not have started as a sole proprietorship but would have incorporated from the outset.

What follows is a quick overview of your options. My aim is to give you enough information so that when you meet with your accountant, tax advisor, and lawyer you at least know what they are talking about. Your specific set of circumstances, however, will determine the correct legal structure for your business. First, a word on taxes.

Taxation

There is a significant difference in the way different structures are taxed. Sole proprietorships and single member limited liability companies (LLCs) are taxed directly to the individual owner on their personal tax return. Multiple member LLCs and S corporations typically file their own separate tax return and issue K-1s to each member/owner, so the net income or loss is typically reflected directly on that individual's personal tax return (though they both have the option to be taxed like a C corporation).

C corporations differ because they must file returns and are taxed independently of the owners of the corporation. Therefore, when profits are distributed to the owners through dividends, those dividends are then taxed on the individuals' tax returns. This is referred to as double taxation of C corporation profits and is the reason many small business owners do not establish a C corporation when starting their business.

It should be noted, however, that recent tax law changes have tried to reduce the discrepancy between the various corporate structures.

Sole Proprietorship

This structure is the least expensive to start or form. One downside is that legal liability is borne directly by the owner. There is no corporate entity to shield liability.

Limited Liability Companies (LLCs)

LLCs can elect to file as either a corporation or a partnership. One advantage is that there is less legal paperwork to establish them when compared to S and C corporations. The legal structure provides the owner some personal legal protection from a lawsuit against the business. LLCs (as compared to C corporations) can be beneficial for active business owners who expect business losses in the early years of the company. The reason being that losses would pass through to the individual's tax return, which could be a benefit if there is other ordinary income to offset. LLC income is subject to self-employment tax.

S Corporations

S corporations can elect to file as either a corporation or a partnership. They can have no more than one hundred shareholders and only one class of stock; other corporations or partnerships are not permitted to own interests, and the IRS scrutinizes distributions to owners as they can be characterized as dividends or salary.

C Corporations

C corporations have no restrictions on the number of shareholders or what type of entity can be a shareholder. However, if the company's total assets exceed $10 million and there are over two thousand investors in total, or five hundred nonaccredited investors (based on the 2016 passage of the Jumpstart Our Business Startups Act [JOBS Act]), the company needs to follow public filing and disclosure rules governed by the Securities and Exchange Commission (SEC). If the owner believes early losses are expected, then those losses would be held up on the tax returns of the corporation and would not flow through to the owner's personal tax return.

Certain tax credits offered by the IRS may only be available to C corporations in a given industry and can't be passed through to an individual through an LLC or an S corporation. This may be important when making your decision as to what legal structure you adopt.

Other Considerations

As I said earlier, the biggest thing is to have an idea of the legal structures open to you and think through how you imagine your business developing over its first few years. For instance, will you be the only owner forever? Do you want to bring in a partner from the beginning, or possibly look for a partner to buy into the business in the future? Will employees be granted ownership as part of their compensation for services? If you have more than one owner, consideration needs to be given to what happens if a member or owner wants to sell or leave. The situation might be handled very differently in an LLC as compared to a C corporation. The operating agreement of the LLC and the buy/sell agreement (if there is more than one member) are critical documents in order to plan for how both expected and unexpected situations will be legally handled in the future.

I have used many of these various entities to grow my businesses. I might form a C corporation because of the use of different shares of stock (preferred stock to the main owner, restricted common stock to key people/executives, then possibly stock options for common stock to other employees). I've used LLCs predominately to take advantage of the early year (active) business losses in order to offset other income.

Now you know the basics, but you might want to do a little more research into legal business structures. My advice is to always go to an expert before making a decision. Talk to your accountant, tax advisor, and lawyer before deciding on your business's legal structure.

Buying a Business

If you've decided you're interested in buying a business, there are business brokers across the country who will show you businesses that are for sale. Remember, a business broker is just like a real estate broker or a car salesperson. They're going to emphasize the positives and not necessarily highlight the negatives. But they could be a good source to help you discover what's available.

Whether you should buy a business or start your own is your decision, but let's discuss what's involved in buying a business. A lot will depend on your financial situation, the industry and market you are looking at entering, the competition, and what opportunities are available. Understanding how to evaluate each opportunity from a risk perspective as well as an investment opportunity is important. The biggest mistake entrepreneurs make when buying a business is not doing enough due diligence.

The Benefits

The biggest benefit of buying an existing company is current revenue and, behind that revenue, a customer base that has hopefully existed over a period of time. This provides a level of predictability— and that's good, very good. Second, you will be able to assess what the company's operating expenses are and see what profit is being earned. Obviously, buying a company that is profitable offers a significant benefit. It's also far more likely you will get the support of banks and other lending institutions for an existing business that is showing a profit than for a far riskier (in their eyes, anyway) start-up.

There is also the possibility the seller might take part in the financing. In other words, if you come up with, say, 25 percent of the purchase price, the seller might take back a promissory note for the balance. It's always worth considering, and obviously it's a matter of negotiation.

Another benefit is the management structure. Having a knowledgeable and experienced management team in place that knows the company's customers, the industry, and the business itself is invaluable.

That is, of course, if they are doing a good job and plan to remain under the new ownership.

Inheriting established employees who are important, or at least somewhat important, to the operation can be a considerable advantage. They're already trained. Based on their tenure, you can probably tell whether the previous owner was happy with them and whether they are quality employees. One of the most important things you should do before making a final decision is to identify which key employees are willing to stay under new ownership. You may want to consider offering an extra incentive package to encourage these people to remain. Remember, losing key players can be detrimental to profitability. Imagine, for instance, what losing the company's top two or three salespeople would do to revenues.

If you purchase a family business, where family members hold a number of critical positions, you may lose your management team once the business transitions to your ownership. Negotiate in advance a transition period during which you can hire replacements who can hopefully be trained by the family.

The benefits of having an existing customer base shouldn't be underestimated. Your market knows your product or service, it is established, and credibility and trust have been earned. You may have to create new products or reinvent others to stimulate sales, but you are not starting at zero when it comes to your customer list and you will also be able to identify your top customers and their buying (and payment) track records.

Due Diligence

When looking to purchase a business, always question why the person is selling. Make no mistake—there is always a reason. It may be obvious. Perhaps they are retiring and have no family to take over the business, or perhaps no one in the family is interested. Many of the more nefarious reasons can often be discovered by a thorough examination of the financial statements.

This is where the quality of the seller's accounting records comes into play. For example, annual sales revenue should be rising or at least staying level. If it's going down, that's a red flag. Same thing with profitability. Another thing people selling businesses like to do, specifically in cash businesses, is inflate the company's revenue by telling would-be purchasers that there is a certain level of cash revenue—revenue that may not be totally reported, or in a worst-case scenario, that may be totally exaggerated. You have to make a value judgment as to the level of that cash business and whether you feel okay doing business that way.

A word of warning: there are some very devious people out there who would love for you to take their ailing business off their hands. Recently one young entrepreneur I'm working with came to me with what he thought was a wonderful opportunity to buy a business. It took only seconds for me to recognize a major concern: the accounts receivable figure was almost 90 percent of total revenues. That percentage is unrealistic, so with minimal digging we discovered that most of the accounts receivable were for inventory that was out on consignment and not actually sold. The question became how much of that product would be sold and how much returned. The lesson? The company was predicting income that may never exist.

Another factor to look at is that owners who have businesses up for sale may have a tendency to inflate the value of their fringe benefits. In other words, they will tell you they get a company car or health benefits. This may well be true, but those benefits are all part of the company's existing profitability. Sellers often overexaggerate how much these benefits are worth.

Advancing Technology

There's one thing that prospective buyers often overlook, and that's an upcoming technology tsunami. Many companies are falling victim to changes in technology that will alter the way they operate or make what they sell obsolete. There are many examples of companies that were thriving but got swept away by new technology they were not prepared for or could not afford to embrace—for instance, those in video rental, music CDs, the yellow pages, payphone franchises, film processing, computer printout paper, and currently, newspapers.

When looking at purchasing a business, consider what is happening to the industry from a technological standpoint. The last thing you want to do is take over a business only to discover you need all new equipment and technology within a year or two.

It's very easy to get caught up in the trappings and glamour of being an entrepreneur, the excitement (and it is exciting) and the exhilaration. Because of it, you may not do a thorough job of looking at the facts. That's where big risk enters the picture.

The Financials

When I consider buying or investing in a business, I have what I call my red-flag checklist. I thoroughly examine the financial statements. The balance sheet, the profit and loss statement, and the cash flow statement all help me decide what I should focus on and the questions I should ask the owner.

My biggest piece of advice is to go through the profit and loss statement line by line and identify exactly what is included under each expense line item. This is the only way you can understand the business intimately.

The Inventory Minefield

Another area of concern when buying a business that includes inventory is its value. The value of existing stock obviously has a major impact on the selling price. If the value is inflated, or a percentage of the stock is outdated and unsellable, you could be in a very dangerous situation.

Not everything in a company's warehouse sells well; some items may be bestsellers, some sell slowly, and others may have been sitting in the warehouse gathering dust for years. Whether it is the former or the latter, you will be paying the same price. As a buyer, you need to know what percentage of the inventory is turning over regularly; that is, what is making a profit and what will end up costing your company money? If 20 percent is unsellable, that's a huge loss you will have to write off. And that's going to affect your profitability right from the outset.

Valuing a Business and Spotting a Good Deal

If you are committed to buying a business, you will want to get the best possible deal. But what is a good deal? Is it a good enough deal money-wise to justify the purchase price?

A return on your equity investment is a major criterion. Quite frankly, I would never invest in or buy somebody's business that didn't give me a good return on my investment. Let me explain that further. If you're trying to establish the value of a business and the business returns a profit every year of, say, $100,000 after owner's compensation, what should you expect to pay for that business? Now, if $100,000 is the profit, and the sale price is $1 million, that's a 10 percent return on your money; if the purchase price were $3 million, that would only be 3 percent.

Personally, I don't think that's enough. I look for 15 to 20 percent as a minimum. Now, if you only paid $500,000, your return would be 20 percent. That return is important, because unless you had cash in hand to make the purchase, you would have to pay off a loan, with interest.

For example, if you paid $2 million for the business and you only made $100,000 profit, which is 5 percent, you might not have enough margin to make your principle and interest payments on the money you borrowed to buy the business.

To put it another way, how long do you want to work before you get your initial investment back? If you're paying $1 million and you're only getting $100,000 of income, you've got to work for ten years until you get your investment back. With this simple thinking, you can start to evaluate the price compared to the profitability of the business.

This method will help you value a business, but there is another factor that could come into play, and that is if you are privilege to some unique knowledge, something you know you can do to make the company grow faster than its current owner or management team has managed to achieve. In this case you might be willing to pay a premium for the company because you know you can exceed that 15 or 20 percent return.

For example, you may be able to create significant economies of scale or there may be some part of the company you can split off into a new division or sell separately. At Paychex, we bought companies on occasion for their software rather than for their business.

Another way you can make a purchase a better deal for you is to spot when a company's expenses are bloated. When you think about value, instead of just seeing the growth of revenue, you might also recognize that there are expenses that could be peeled away to immediately enhance the company's bottom line. Some owners have little control over their expenses, and a new owner with a sharp pencil can increase bottom-line profit quite easily and effectively.

Buying a Franchise

Franchises are another area of business opportunity with their own advantages and disadvantages. Buying a franchise could be right for you, but there are a great number of factors you should take into consideration.

On the positive side, you generally have a product that has a good track record, and it can be measured against the success of other franchisees. The franchisor provides a proven pattern for operation or management, and they are there to assist you in finding the right location and provide training for both you and your employees.

On the negative side, they may limit your ability to make product changes or enhancements; to franchisors there is value in consistency. Unfortunately, this may restrict your options when it comes to product definition. In addition, you will almost certainly have to pay them a continuing royalty, a cost that has to be built into your business expenses.

Before deciding to purchase a franchise, be very confident in the brand you're choosing; after all, you are putting all your eggs into that particular basket. Consumers have a lot of choice, and that creates risk, especially if you're not choosing a well-established name.

The first thing you should do if you're contemplating purchasing a franchise is to talk to other franchisees and ask about any concerns they might have about their franchisor. Do your due diligence. Ask what issues they have faced and how they were dealt with by the franchisor. Generally speaking, franchisees will more than likely be happy to talk to you and will give you honest feedback and firsthand knowledge.

Buying a Job

There are certain businesses that offer little or no return on investment but do provide the owner with a regular income. These are often one-person businesses, such as a small retail store or perhaps a consultancy. Buying a business like this offers the owner a great deal of independence without the responsibility of managing employees.

For instance, let's say you want to realize an annual income of $100,000. You can certainly purchase a business that will generate that salary for you. The challenge is, there may not be enough profit left over to give you a return on your investment. Basically, you have bought yourself a job. It may not be a good investment, but people do it all the time. The reason, of course, is the freedom of working for oneself, not having to report to anyone, and not having a boss. Psychologically this can be very important to some people, and they might eventually be able to sell the business to someone else and get their investment back, but there is, as with all business ventures, a level of risk involved. However, as I said in the opening chapter, there is also risk in having a job.

Takeaways

- The viability of a business can be shown on a one-page profit and loss projection, which shows you immediately what you have to do to turn a profit.
- No one is going to read a thirty-thousand-word business plan. Focus on the key points and financials that demonstrate your business concept is viable and cut the rest of the verbiage.

UNDERSTAND YOUR BUSINESS

- The most important thing when planning your business should be the accuracy of your facts and statistics. Don't let passion cloud your judgment.
- A first-rate business plan can often tell you *not* to start the business at all but to run away fast.
- Understanding every aspect of your business is of paramount importance when talking to lenders and investors.
- Consider how you plan to grow your business and whether you will want to bring on board investors or partners, or sell shares later.
- Choosing the correct business structure from the outset will save you money and taxes and may protect you from legal issues down the road.
- Consult a lawyer, an accountant, and a tax advisor before deciding on the best legal structure for your business.
- Buying a business is a valid way of becoming an entrepreneur, but be careful and carry out due diligence.

THREE

MONEY MATTERS

People often ask me, "How can I start a business when I don't have enough money?" My advice? *Don't.* Too many businesses start out undercapitalized, and it's downhill all the way from there. What makes things worse is that banks don't like lending money to small businesses. So what are your options if you still want to start out on your own or take your business to the next level?

You may decide to go out and look for private funding, but I'll warn you, there's a skill to going after investors. First, you need a quality presentation and a solid plan. You then need people (prospects) to whom you can present your concept. You also need to be smart about what you ask for and what you intend to do with the money. Also, if you do raise outside capital for an existing business, you have disclosure responsibilities to your shareholders, either legally or ethically.

How Much Money Do You Need?

I went four years without getting a paycheck from Paychex. That's the reality of starting a business. And I wasn't laughing at the irony, I assure you. The reality is that financing won't be easy to come by, and it won't come to you; you'll have to go out and knock on doors to make it happen.

Before you begin, do some simple arithmetic: estimate your operating costs for the first year, add whatever you need to pay yourself (zero is a good number), and then figure out how many widgets or services you need to sell to cover that amount. This will give you a baseline of your financial requirements. Look at the quantity of products or services you need to sell and assess whether it's reasonable. If it isn't, reduce it to what you believe will be achievable. You may now be showing a loss. These basic numbers do not take into account *when* you will need access to cash to pay for capital expenditures and other overhead expenses. You should take your cash requirements into consideration before coming up with the amount you need to either launch your new venture or grow your existing business.

Sources of Financing

Self-Financing

If you can finance your business without borrowing money or bringing in investors, all the better. If you truly believe in your business concept, whether it's a start-up or a going concern that requires investment, you should seriously consider liquidating personal assets to self-finance. The way I look at it, if you are asking other people to risk their money, or in the case of banks, their customers' money, then you should feel comfortable risking your own.

Take a close look at your assets: real estate, stocks, bonds, potentially even your 401(k). It's not uncommon for entrepreneurs to sell their Harley-Davidson motorcycle, a baseball card collection, or a signed football. Interestingly, a baseball signed by the original eleven baseball

Hall of Famers recently sold for almost $630,000—that could have been the answer to an entrepreneur's immediate funding requirements.

All my partners and franchisees in the early days of Paychex were employees of institutions or companies, and none of them, to my knowledge, had run a business before. Although they started with me in Rochester, they moved across the country to open offices, funding their new businesses through the sale of their homes. A few borrowed from family and friends.

Put Your Money Where Your Mouth Is

If you're not willing to invest money in your own business, then you might want to reconsider your options. Sorry to be brutally honest, but the most help I can give you is a reality check before you go too much further. As I suggested earlier, it's unrealistic to expect an investor or a bank to invest in your business or lend you money while *you* are protecting your own personal assets. Why should *they* take all the financial risk? You have to believe in your enterprise. If you aren't willing to put a second mortgage on your house or sell your boat, it's going to be difficult to convince an investor to give you start-up capital and almost impossible to get a bank to give you an unsecured loan or line of credit.

Sweat Equity

There's a big difference between sweat equity with no capital and sweat equity with capital and the value of that equity (perceived or otherwise). Some investors put a higher value on sweat equity than others, but all like to see you have some skin in the game.

Banks

Generally, banks are reluctant to lend to small businesses, especially to start-ups. They will, however, consider lending money if you have liquid, pledged collateral (for example, a stock certificate that is easily saleable) or if you get a first or second mortgage on your home. They may also require someone to cosign a loan, and that person will need to be someone of substance.

Building a strong relationship with your bank manager is important; it played an important part in the funding of Paychex over the years. In fact, my first bank officer, Tom Clark, became Paychex's chief financial officer.

When I first started Paychex, I was forced to take a second mortgage on my home, and I also managed to get some consumer loans, thanks to understanding loan managers. These loans were ostensibly for consolidating personal debt but were in fact used to finance my company. As an entrepreneur you have to raise money wherever you can, and sometimes you have to be creative.

Coincidentally, those same loan managers came to a Paychex annual meeting recently, and although they're now long retired, I recognized them and introduced them to the gathering. I told everyone that these guys went out on a limb for me in the early 1970s to help me keep my Paychex dream alive.

The Bank of Mom and Pop

Approaching your parents and other family members is a valid way to raise capital, but it comes with baggage. They know you too well and are more likely to question how you are running the business. And they won't be shy about asking for their money back if they need it for something else. They are sometimes not the most educated of lenders.

I used this particular "bank" myself in the very early days of Paychex, and without it the company may not have survived. We were developing new software to run payrolls, and we got to a point where I didn't have the money to continue paying the developers. Without an immediate influx of cash, we were going to be in serious trouble. I talked to my sister, Marie, and she offered me whatever I needed from the insurance benefit she had received when her husband passed away. I borrowed $30,000 from her; without it I doubt Paychex would exist today. Family can often come through for you when your back is against the wall. As a result of her generosity, Marie and her three children became significant shareholders in Paychex.

Country-Club Capital

Selling shares to friends and acquaintances is a bona fide way of raising start-up capital. It can be effective, but it's not without its pitfalls. People will ask when and how they can get their money out and what the return on investment will be. Tough questions. Then, if something does go wrong, you have to consider how it might affect your reputation in the community.

Venture Capital

Venture capitalists can be an option, but they are self-centered, tough negotiators with their own agendas. They want to invest and then liquidate, so their timeline might be very different from yours. If you are trying to build something long-term, you have to ensure the venture capitalists you are working with are on the same page. Another thing to beware of is that they may take advantage of the fact you might need funding urgently and use it against you when negotiating terms.

Going Public

Public offerings have become less popular in the last decade for several reasons, the primary one being that federal regulations have made it very difficult and very expensive to run a public company. Utilizing venture capital is a lot less expensive.

There are many reasons, however, why it's beneficial to take a company public. One of the biggest is the ability to raise money for capital expenses such as new hardware, computers, and the like. It also offers liquidity for shareholders, who then have the opportunity to buy or sell shares whenever they want. They also have the freedom to sell as many or as few as they like, although there are restrictions on what are called insiders (board members and senior management), whose level of buying and selling activity is monitored by the SEC.

Going public is good for marketing. If you're a public company your name is out there, and it provides a high degree of credibility. It makes recruitment of high-quality employees easier as they are more likely to seek you out when you have a high-profile name. You are also seen to have substance and permanence, as opposed, for example, to a privately owned family company that can be viewed as being more volatile. Prospective employees also realize they may be able to take advantage of stock options and other benefits.

There are downsides, of course. You and your CFO have to commit yourselves to dealing with Wall Street on a regular basis. Wall Street will be concerned with consistency; it doesn't like ups and downs, and it can be difficult to run a business like that.

My suggestion is to get a lot of advice and counsel before embarking on a course that leads to a public offering.

Taking Paychex Public

Let me share with you a little of the excitement I felt when I took Paychex public. My criterion for going public was based on the company reaching a seven-figure or $1 million post-tax bottom line. By the middle of 1983, Paychex had not only reached that milestone but also had twenty-five thousand clients and five hundred employees. I felt at that point we were established enough and would generate sufficient interest and support for the company stock that I would be comfortable going public.

With the decision made, all I had to do was make it happen. I remember it was Friday morning, August 26, 1983, twelve years after I started the company, and the market was at the tail end of a bubble. My advisors and I had to decide on the price per share; we were looking at between $11 and $13, which would have given us a market cap (outstanding shares multiplied by market price) of about $65 million. How it worked was that we got the range and then the investment guys ran around to their institutional customers trying to stimulate interest.

Bob Beegen, my midwestern partner, and I were in Rochester, and our chief financial officer and our lawyer were in New York. Along with some seasoned board members, we were all on the phone with the investment banker and he said, "Tom, the price is $11." I wasn't quite sure how I felt about that, so I put them on hold to talk to Bob privately. Although I had muted my voice, I could still hear everyone else on the line. The conversation was illuminating; I heard the others say that the act of going public was more important than the specific value at which the initial share price was set. That made sense to me, and I was confident the share value would rise as interest in the stock grew. Therefore, based on the information we had at that time, we went public at the recommended $11 a share. Consequently, as expected, the figure rose steadily, and we raised $7.7 million, which we mainly invested in new computer hardware.

I liked running a public company, in part because I enjoyed working in an environment of discipline and structure. Institutional investors are mostly concerned about growth, but that growth has to have predictability. As I said earlier, they don't like hills and valleys;

they look for steady, consistent growth. Fortunately, Paychex was a company that demonstrated very predictable growth.

As CEO of Paychex, I made a lot of friends in the investment analyst community, and I enjoyed working with them. Too many CEOs seem to resent that community, primarily because analysts are very inquisitive. The less predictable your company, the more difficult they make your life. And that is reflected in a fluctuating stock price. The more consistent and predictable your company's profits are, the easier it is for analysts to recommend working with your company and to recommend your company to their institutional shareholders.

Stock analysis is a very important part of a CEO's day-to-day activity. Public companies must have a CEO and CFO who like working with analytic institutions because they can make or break you as far as your stock price is concerned. If the analysts don't have a high level of trust and confidence in your company, and in you personally, they are not going to be kind to you.

Wherever you get your funding from, never lose sight of the fact that your investors eventually want to see a return of their capital along with a return on their investment. This return can be delivered via dividends or capital gains from the selling of shares.

When you have outside shareholders, the percentage of ownership is a major issue for negotiation. You may find yourself in a position where you have to sell more shares, and this will, of course, change your ownership percentage.

Understanding Financial Statements

Shortly after I purchased the Buffalo Sabres hockey team, I remember Larry Quinn, the CEO, laughing at my ruler because it had a magnifying glass embedded into its entire length. I still have it, and I still use it. It enables me to focus line by line as I study a spreadsheet, something I find exceptionally useful. I used it to look at the Sabres' financial statements. Larry was amazed that I went over every line in such detail. It also came in handy when I cornered President Bill Clinton in my box at a Sabres game to go through a conference budget when I was founding sponsor and underwriter of the Clinton Global Initiative.

If you don't understand financial statements, you are running your business blindfolded. I think many entrepreneurs get into trouble simply because they don't understand their financial statements, of which the balance sheet and the profit and loss statement are the most important.

As we discussed earlier, profit and loss statements, balance sheets, and cash flow statements are vital to keeping your finger on the pulse of your business. Too often businesspeople run their businesses on a cash basis—in other words, they focus on their bank balance: if that is healthy, then they feel all is right with the business. I never get involved with a business that operates this way. In my opinion every entrepreneur should take a basic accounting course and learn the fundamentals of good accounting practice.

People get scared by the numbers. If you feel mathematics is not your strong suit, don't worry; understanding your business's finances requires nothing more than simple arithmetic. After all, if you can learn the basics of a program such as Microsoft Excel, it will do all the calculations for you. Most entrepreneurs avoid the numbers behind their business—but to me, it's where I discover all the answers.

I'm a numbers guy, and it has served me well, very well, over the years. If you know your numbers, you know your business. Any entrepreneur who does not understand financial statements is in great danger.

The Balance Sheet

A balance sheet is a snapshot of your business at a set moment in time. Your balance sheet shows your assets (cash, accounts receivable, inventory, prepaid expenses, furniture, equipment, etc.) and liabilities (accounts payable, unpaid expenses, etc.). If you take your assets and subtract your liabilities, you have your company's net worth. Your net worth contains the profits you have made and money you or your shareholders have invested. This snapshot can be taken at any time.

The Profit and Loss Statement

We went over this in chapter 2, but as a reminder, this document is sometimes called an income statement and is a recap (either for a month, a quarter, or a year) of all the revenue you brought into the company and all the expenses you incurred in maintaining the company. The difference between the two is either your profit or your loss.

Cash Flow Spreadsheet of Forecast

A cash flow forecast predicts the company's monthly revenue and expenses over a period of time, usually twelve months. It shows your monthly opening bank balance, revenues, expenses, and monthly closing balance. Revenue predictions are usually based on your sales forecasts. A cash flow forecast is a useful tool both for monitoring your company's performance and for identifying your cash requirements ahead of time.

Managing Your Financials

It's important to have someone who understands financial statements in your company, someone who knows how to read them and how to prepare them. You can get into a lot of trouble with bankers and investors if your financials are not reconciled and up to date. More importantly, without accurate current financials you won't have a realistic view of your business's financial situation.

Many mature businesses will have outside auditors audit their financial statements annually, but if your company is smaller you should at least have an accounting firm carry out an overview of your financial statements every year.

One last thing: you should never take for granted that your financial statements are correct. People make mistakes, so your statements can be wrong. Have someone you trust, a good financial person, look after your financials.

Understanding Profitability

The primary reason you are running a company is to make money. You owe it to your shareholders, your investors, your staff, your customers, the charitable organizations you support, and yourself to make money—and you can't do that if you are not making a net profit. I know that sounds obvious, but I come across entrepreneurs all the time who can't explain their company's financial situation, including how much profit they're making. They refer me to their financial statements, but when I ask questions, they look at me blankly, as if I'm speaking a foreign language.

Understanding profit margins is essential to the overall health of your company. I'm now going to share with you the whole essence of Paychex's impressive profitability by first asking you a question. The underlying lessons in this story can apply to a wide range of companies selling both products and services.

So, the question: If you are a payroll processor, would you rather service ten 10-person company payrolls or one 100-person company payroll?

The answer may surprise you. It's better to service ten 10-person company payrolls. That may sound counterintuitive at first, but here's why: clients with a large number of employees and therefore paychecks per pay period pay less per check than a small company with only a handful of employees. This principle holds true in many industries: the larger the purchase, the higher the discount.

Back to Paychex . . . Servicing ten 10-person payrolls grosses 2.5 times more revenue than one 100-person payroll. You are probably thinking this will be offset by an increase in overhead costs in dealing with ten customers rather than just one. In reality, I assure you, the additional overhead is not proportional to the additional revenue.

You may also be considering that it must be tougher to make ten sales than just one. On the face of it, that would appear to be the case, but again, this requires further investigation. First, a 100-person payroll company is harder to sell to because usually it has someone on staff already handling its payroll demands. In addition, larger companies can be more demanding and more price conscious.

Second, believe it or not, it's easier to sell ten 10-person payrolls than a single 100-person payroll. Although, admittedly, that has changed a little in recent years for Paychex. Back when I started my company, everyone was ignoring the small guys, so I had the market virtually to myself. Today, due to the Paychex approach, increasing numbers of payroll processors now target small business owners, so the competition is far stiffer.

It was this basic principle that EAS (the first company I worked for in payroll processing) didn't understand when I tried to sell them the idea of opening up the small business market. Maybe I didn't push it hard enough, but I always knew there was a massive opportunity hidden in that math. Could this approach offer you a new target market?

To prove the validity of this profit-margin lesson, here we are almost fifty years later, and Paychex's pretax profit is around 38 percent, while ADP's is about 19 percent. The reason? Our revenue per check is much higher. The lesson here is that the best route to higher profitability is not always the most obvious.

It's this counterintuitive approach to business, and my constant questioning of the way things have always been done, that I want to share with you in this book. Don't always believe common business lore. In this case we explored the concept that it takes more work and is less profitable to cobble together a bunch of small customers than to land one large client. It's not always true. Question commonly held beliefs every time.

Pricing

One of the problems entrepreneurs face is determining the price of their product. A lot depends on the cost of production and the price your competitors are charging. The concern is always: Are you selling your product at a high enough price to allow the margin between the sale price and your costs for that product to cover all the rest of your expenses? In some businesses the margin is not high enough and therefore they will never be profitable.

The challenge is that sometimes the market won't bear a higher price and if you raise it too high, sales will drop. This becomes a balancing act between revenues and expenses. If you can't justify increasing your prices, you will need to take a long, hard look at your production costs.

Get a Pre- or Postnuptial

Whenever people ask me what the first thing is that they should do when they start a business, I don't skip a beat. I say, "Get a prenup!" Sure, they all laugh, but then I repeat myself. "I'm serious, get a prenup."

A concern any entrepreneur should have is that, unfortunately, relationships don't always last, and here I am talking primarily about marital relationships of any type, including common-law. Life happens, and people change and divorce and separate. In fact, it's becoming increasingly common.

Without a prenuptial, if you own a business and you're in a community property state, you may be faced with a situation where you have to sell your business to make a settlement with your spouse. If you find yourself in that situation, there are a couple of major downsides over and above the obvious. First, you may not be able to get the price you want for your business because you are under pressure to sell immediately, and second—I know this seems obvious, but hear me out—if you sell your business, you don't have it anymore. Think about it. All of a sudden you have lost your source of income.

If you start your business and you are already married, you can get a postnuptial agreement that outlines what would happen with regard to the business should one of you want to take a different direction in life.

There is nothing more serious than protecting your ideas, your investments, and your business from day one. I have seen many great entrepreneurs and businesses disappear because a relationship went south. From the outset you have to protect yourself and your business. You have to make it a major priority.

Takeaways

- If you don't have sufficient capital to safely start your business, don't.
- If you don't have enough seed money to begin the process of starting your own company, find a creative way to raise it.
- Never underestimate the potential of the bank of mom and pop and country-club capital. But as with all business arrangements, ensure all parties understand the terms and get everything in writing.
- Be realistic about how much capital you require. Do the simple arithmetic.
- Be willing to invest your own money and assets in your business before asking lenders and investors to risk their money.
- Be prepared not to take a paycheck for a period of time.
- Be clear as to how investment capital will be used and be aware of investor expectations.
- Venture capitalists have vastly different goals than business owners.
- Don't approach investors or lenders without a professional and realistic business plan.
- Prepare a professional presentation when approaching potential investors.
- Realize the true value of sweat equity—it's not what you

perceive it to be; it's what an investor perceives it to be.

- Going public can be beneficial, but it is not for everyone.
- If you don't understand financial statements, you are running your business blindfolded.
- Never take for granted that your financial statements are correct. People make mistakes, so they can be wrong. Have someone you trust, a good financial person, look after your financials.
- Understanding profit margins is essential to the overall health of your company.
- Get a prenuptial or postnuptial agreement.

FOUR

WOULD YOU BUY
WHAT YOU SELL?

The one thing companies have in common is that they all sell something, a product or a service. But how important is what you sell to your long-term success?

In some cases, people choose to sell a product or service or to become part of an industry because they have a passion for it. Think of all the geeks who create hi-tech products that they hope will change the way people work or play, or even help solve global issues. Others choose products or services based on what they themselves like to consume, things that excite them. Still others find, or think they have found, a gap in the market and aim to fill an unmet need or demand.

In addition to the actual product or service you sell, it's important to take notice that there are two types of business formats: recurring and nonrecurring revenue businesses. I am a fan of the former. Let me tell you why.

In the late 1960s and early '70s, I found myself working as a salesman for a payroll processing company, not because I had a passion for the industry, but to earn enough money to support my family. Payroll processing, on the face of it, is not a very exciting business, but I soon learned that it offered the ability to sell a service to a customer and then repeatedly deliver that same service week after week, month after month, year after year to that same customer. That proposition excited me. If you sell a sofa to a customer, it may be decades before they need another one, and by the time they do, they have probably forgotten you exist. Even if they do come back to you, you have to sell them all over again in the face of competition for their dollar.

When Paychex starts handling a company's payroll, it keeps providing the service until for some reason the customer no longer needs or wants the service. You can count on the revenue; it's very predictable. Paychex has been handling payroll for some of its customers for several decades. That sort of stability is appreciated by banks and investors and, if you go public, Wall Street.

Not only is the recurring revenue predictable, so is future growth. If you add a hundred new clients, you can easily calculate the revenue they will generate. That level of predictability and consistency is not available to many nonrecurring revenue businesses. I like predictability; it helps me sleep at night.

Another example of a successful recurring revenue business is a sports franchise. When I purchased the Buffalo Sabres in 2003, we had 5,800 season ticket holders. We grew that to over 15,000, and there was a waiting list. Having that predictable revenue helped enormously with stabilizing the franchise.

Recurring revenue businesses don't have to be service based. There are plenty of examples of businesses that sell products that manage to create recurring revenue streams. Have you ever had drinking water delivered to your house? That's a recurring revenue business. Even companies selling software have, in recent years, strategically changed the way they do business to encourage recurring revenue by selling monthly subscriptions to their software rather than selling a single download or a disc containing the program. Locking in customers is the genius of this type of business model. As long as your customers remain happy with what you are selling them, they will continue to pay you monthly, quarterly, or annually, and they are sheltered from the attention of your competitors.

Six Key Questions

Whatever the reason behind your choice of business, you must choose wisely if you expect your company to be successful. Here are six questions I encourage you to ask yourself about the products or services you are either selling now or planning to sell in the future.

1. Is there a large enough market?
2. Can you make a decent profit margin?
3. Can your company deliver?
4. Does it have longevity?
5. Do you have enough capital?
6. Can you keep up with technological change?

Let's break down each of these questions.

Is There a Large Enough Market?

Is there a large enough market for the product or service you are selling? Often entrepreneurs simply assume there is a market large enough to create sufficient revenues and profit to cover a business's overhead.

This overconfidence can be dangerous. I've even heard people say things like, "They'll be lining up to buy this as soon as we open our doors." I can tell you that in all my years in business I've never seen that happen for a new business or a new product. Sure, if you are Apple and you're launching a new iPhone or iPad there may well be lineups, but Apple has been around for a long time and has built a massively large and loyal consumer base.

My initial goal when I launched Paychex was to sign up three hundred clients. This target was based on the personal revenue I required to maintain a decent lifestyle. I was confident I could achieve this fairly quickly. In reality it took four years.

I remember my first direct mail-out. I sent it to just about every potential prospect in Rochester. I co-opted my nephews and nieces, and they came in to seal envelopes, lick postage stamps, and do whatever else was needed to launch my first marketing venture. We sent out the mailing on December 15, 1970. The end result was that between the direct mail campaign and paying my only employee, I burned through my total investment within the first six weeks of operation. I was hoping to acquire sixty clients from the mail-out—I got six. Three thousand direct mail pieces and all I got was a lousy 0.2 percent return on my investment. Right away I knew I was in trouble.

That's often the way with entrepreneurs. I've sat through pitches where a new business owner has a great idea and declares they can capture 10 percent of the market. It's never that easy. Never. Today, of course, Paychex signs two thousand new clients a week, but that's the difference between a start-up and a company that's been around for over forty years.

Overestimating the market is a perennial problem for entrepreneurs; optimism is built into their genes. This, of course, is a double-edged sword. In general terms, optimism is a good trait for an entrepreneur; otherwise, they would never consider starting a business. But overoptimism leads to inflated revenue expectations, which never materialize and subsequently endanger the entire business. I'm certainly not immune to this entrepreneur's disease. Let me tell you the story of when I jumped into a business without doing enough due diligence and market research.

The business I invested in was a dental imaging clinic. The concept was simple: many dentists at that time didn't have sophisticated imaging equipment for people requiring complicated dental procedures or cosmetic surgery, so we provided the images to allow them to carry out the work. We were certain they would line up at our door once we opened our clinic. Why wouldn't they?

Well, it turned out not enough dentists were willing to send their patients to an external service. Bottom line: we couldn't get enough dentists to send us their patients, to make the company financially viable.

Depending on which report or study you read, approximately 80 percent of consumer products fail. I hope that convinces you not to believe your own press and to carry out sufficient market research. You need to accurately estimate the size of your potential market and the cost of getting a high enough percentage of that market through your door.

Can You Make a Decent Profit Margin?

Whatever product or service you provide, you have to ensure you can make a profit every time you sell a unit. That sounds obvious, but I've come across businesspeople who say they understand this but then can't tell me off the top of their heads what their gross profit margin is on the items or services they sell.

In its simplest form, your gross profit margin is what you can sell something for minus what it costs you to produce the item. The gross profit on everything you sell has to be sufficient to cover your corporate overhead.

Your variable costs are for raw materials, manufacturing, distribution, license fees, and any direct labor costs (e.g., piecework costs, etc.). Variable costs are costs that you incur when you sell something, unlike fixed costs (e.g., rent), which you incur regardless of whether you sell something.

You need to not only make a profit on each item or service you sell, but that profit when multiplied by the total number of units you sell needs to generate enough revenue to cover all your overhead (i.e., fixed costs).

Making a suitable gross profit margin can be a balancing act between the price you can charge and the cost of delivering the product or service. To obtain a higher profit margin, you have two options: raise your price or reduce your costs. If you find yourself in a position where, because of competitive pressure, you cannot charge more and there is no way to reduce your variable costs, your product or service may not be a viable proposition. Making that discovery *before* you launch your company will save you a lot of money.

One area some entrepreneurs fail to take full advantage of is negotiating lower prices on raw materials and finding creative ways to reduce manufacturing and production costs. Being resourceful when sourcing raw materials or other variable costs is a key way to increase the profit on each item.

Can Your Company Deliver?

How complicated is it to manufacture your product or deliver your service? Before you commit, ensure you have looked at every step of the production process. Not only do you need to have vendors and key employees lined up, but you also need a backup strategy should a supplier let you down. Carry out a risk analysis by considering everything that could go wrong. What, for instance, will you do if there is a shortage of your primary raw material and not only does it become difficult to obtain but the market price rises to a point where it seriously affects your profit margin? Do you have room to raise your price without it affecting sales? How vulnerable is your profit margin? How can you minimize that vulnerability?

Does It Have Longevity?

I've heard it said that over three-quarters of the products that were around just five years ago no longer exist. Certainly, over the years we have seen technology make obsolete a large number of once-popular products and services. But it's not only new science that changes what consumers want to buy; new generations have different expectations, and trends such as environmental awareness and an increasing reliance on cellular communication affect what and how people buy. Gluten-free products were all but unheard of a few years ago but today are big sellers. The question is whether this is a fad or a range of products that are here to stay. This applies to a wide range of products and services.

When you look at introducing a new product or service to the market, think ten years into the future and try to figure out whether it could be prone to extinction. For instance, is this a good time to start a newspaper, open a camera retail store, or manufacture e-readers? Probably not. Consumer products and services have a shelf life, some longer than others. Choose one with a longer shelf life.

Do You Have Enough Capital?

Many businesses start out undercapitalized. As I mentioned earlier, I started Paychex with only $3,000 and a credit card, which was soon cut in half by a restaurant owner under the instruction of American Express, so who am I to talk? You can bootstrap a business, but you are reducing your chances of success significantly.

My advice? Do your homework. Get a decent calculator, or these days a decent app on your phone, and do the math. Get help to ensure you have thought of every dime you will need to get you through the first year or more. Figure how much you need to sell and be honest; put your optimism aside for this exercise and keep it real. Then you will need to figure out how you are going to raise the necessary capital. In chapter 3, "Money Matters," I provided an overview of your options.

Can You Keep Up with Technological Change?

The speed of technological change is astounding and accelerating every year. If your product or service is in any way reliant on technology, you need to be aware of the capital costs involved in constantly updating what you sell or what you use to manufacture what you sell. And it's not only the cost of reinventing the wheel regularly; consider the time, effort, and money required to continually promote and sell new versions of products. Finally, when products become outdated, they clog your warehouse with unsold and potentially unsellable inventory that can be a significant drain on your bottom line.

Product Diversification

An important milestone in Paychex's history was the moment Gene Polisseni, my best friend and HR director, and his associate Tony Tortorella walked into my office and told me we should be selling 401(k) administration. They outlined a well-defined plan and I liked the idea. As was the case with most of our previous entries into new sectors, everything had to be done manually, until we had time to develop the appropriate software programs. It was this development that led us into other products, such as workers' compensation insurance, employee handbooks, and a menu of other human resource services. Today, Paychex has revenue of over $1.8 billion in payroll services and over $1.5 billion in HR services annually.

These new services were important to our growth in the late '90s because they were a win-win for Paychex and its clients. We could offer these products at a lower cost than our competitors while still making a good profit. They were profitable because we linked two products together. We could, for example, process 150,000 payroll clients on a Monday, and if 50,000 of them had a 401(k) plan, we had the work and administration done and the money in the investor's hands by 6:00 a.m. on Tuesday. The other huge benefit was our level of accuracy. Because we processed the payroll, what was on the 401(k) reports reflected exactly what was in the payroll. This gave us a tremendous advantage over our competition. Today, Paychex sells a larger number of new 401(k) plans every year than any other company. The HR Services division is growing in double digits annually.

Always be on the lookout for ways to diversify your product range, especially by using what you already have in different ways or by piggybacking products.

How Multiple Product-Related Mistakes Can Kill a Business

I hope you are beginning to see the challenges you will face when you consider, and ultimately decide on, what you want to sell. But fear not, there's nothing difficult in increasing the odds that what you sell will make you a profit; you just need to carry out the due diligence outlined above.

I'll leave you with a final story of a business I invested in that made several product-related mistakes. It ended up in bankruptcy, but it all could have been avoided by keeping to the no-nonsense rules I promote throughout this book.

Bak USA was started as a social enterprise, which in this case meant putting job creation above profitability, a dangerous thing to do. In my opinion, businesses should focus on making a profit first, and once they are successful, then look at social enterprise opportunities. Bak manufactured computer tablets. One was extra tough and rugged for use on construction jobsites and other environments where a normal tablet probably wouldn't survive its first day; the other was a two-in-one tablet built for classroom and business use. Both were good products, but the profits were never large enough to give the company a sufficient margin to allow it to deal with the constant need for upgrading and technical improvements.

Bak had one other major problem: their biggest customer, Microsoft, accounted for 90 percent of their business. As the company's largest buyer, it received a discount, which meant Bak's profit margin fell to only 10 percent of their wholesale price. I talk in more detail about the dangers of relying on one or two major customers for the bulk of your revenue in chapter 5.

It was a perfect storm. They couldn't raise their price, selling more was not going to help the situation, and not only could they not lower production-related costs, those costs were in fact increasing due to changing technology. All this while trying to operate like a flourishing Silicon Valley company before they were financially stable.

Never let products and services just happen. Think long and hard about all the issues we've discussed in this chapter and you will make decisions that will lead your company to a healthy and profitable future.

Takeaways

- Recurring revenue businesses offer better opportunities for sustainable sales than nonrecurring revenue businesses.
- Never assume there is a market large enough to create sufficient revenues and profit to cover your business's overhead.
- Always be aware of your gross profit margin and understand what revenues you need to cover costs and also make a profit.
- Overconfidence in your product or service can be dangerous.
- It's not good enough to simply have a good product or service; you need to be able to deliver what you sell consistently and reliably.
- Over 75 percent of products that were around five years ago no longer exist. Ensure your product can stand the test of time.

BUILT, NOT BORN

- Technological change can sometimes be like an incoming tsunami.
- Always be on the lookout for ways to diversify your product range, especially by using what you already have in different ways or by piggybacking products.

FIVE

IT'S NOT A CASH FLOW PROBLEM—IT'S A SALES PROBLEM

What do I mean when I say it's a sales problem, not a cash flow problem? I think the biggest mistake entrepreneurs make is they have a tendency to overestimate their ability to sell their product or service. Once they open their doors or hang their shingle, they believe the world will beat a path to their door. Take it from me, that just does not happen. Today, Paychex brings on board more than a thousand new clients a week, but as I said earlier, it took me four years to get my first three hundred!

When entrepreneurs overestimate their company's potential sales, they are doing the same thing with their gross revenue. This results in a cash flow problem. In simple terms, there is not enough cash coming into the business to pay the company's overhead. So they go to the bank and report that they have a cash flow problem, but in reality, it's a sales problem. Or, if we look at the bigger picture, a management problem.

In short, if your business is short of cash, the first place to look is at your sales productivity. Assuming you've done your budgeting correctly and you aren't spending all your money on exotic cars and . . . well, whatever, then your operating costs should be under control.

Hopefully you also have a cash flow spreadsheet that details what revenues your company needs to achieve to meet your monthly outgoing obligations. Linked to this document, you should have a sales forecast spreadsheet, showing targets and actual sales for each salesperson. I'll discuss this later in this chapter.

Because administrative staff are not part of the selling process, the importance of the sales department is often underestimated. If you're the CEO, however, you need to know at all times whether your sales revenues are on target. If they aren't, your financial situation can deteriorate extremely rapidly.

Understanding Sales

Here is a fundamental truth: nothing happens in a company until someone sells something. The importance of the act of selling something frequently gets lost in business school curriculum, where it is usually combined with marketing. But there's a difference between sales and marketing; knowing that difference is an important first step in creating a sales strategy. Academic programs often fail to discuss the act of *selling*; that is, the personal interaction between a salesperson and a prospect. The act of selling and the art of negotiation are imperative to every business on the planet. It doesn't matter what your business is; someone has to sell something.

When you employ my philosophy of no-nonsense business, you will realize that you are the best person to sell your product (initially, at least). There is nothing better than experiencing firsthand the objections prospects have for not buying what you are selling and learning how to handle those objections. You'll also gain an understanding of what motivates your buyers. Once you've experienced the sales process yourself, you can share the knowledge you have gained with your sales team and give them a clear idea of what they are going to hear when they're face-to-face with prospects. There is no one better than you to train your sales management and salespeople. Let's face it, entrepreneurs: it's imperative you learn to sell your product or service and, more importantly, how to be productive at it.

Before You Make a Sale, You Need Prospects

There are many different ways to sell a product or service, so developing an effective sales strategy that identifies key prospects is vital. There are plenty of books dedicated to the art and science of prospecting, so I'm not going to give you a lesson here on how to fill your pipeline, or sales funnel, or whatever. What I will say is that you need to be creative when figuring out how to reach customers in your target market, and you need to solve the prospecting riddle early on in the game.

In the early days of Paychex, I realized CPAs (certified public accountants) didn't actually want to process payrolls for their clients; it was too much work for too little reward. This turned out to be a major discovery. Uncovering this simple fact enabled me to work through them to reach out to their clients. My initial direct mail strategy may have had limited success, but working with CPAs was hugely successful. More than forty years later, it is still the way Paychex sells many of its customers.

Beware Sleeping with Elephants

If you are out there prospecting and you come across a potentially huge customer, be cautious. You have to be careful when selling to what I call elephants. The "elephant" in this case is any major customer that accounts for a sizeable percentage of your overall sales revenue. These clients appear very attractive, and they can be; however, they come with some baggage. Here are several challenges you will face if you focus on these "highly desirable" prospects and customers.

First, they can take a long time to close, and you will face stiff competition for their business. Second, they are not usually as profitable as you might expect. Large, important clients expect heavy discounts, and as I mentioned, your competitors will also be trying to get their business, so beware of a race to the bottom when it comes to profit margins. You need to ask yourself whether high revenues, low profit is a good strategy for your company.

One final danger is that you will likely have to increase your overhead to allow you to build capacity in order to service an elephant, or elephants; then, sometime later, should they decide to change supplier, you will be left with increased overhead with no corresponding revenue. Losing one or more major customers on which you rely heavily for a large percentage of your gross revenues can quickly, and sometimes unexpectedly, throw you into treacherous financial waters.

Here's a little-known fact: Paychex doesn't have any customer that accounts for more than 1/1000th of its total revenue. That puts the company not only in a very strong position but in a predictable one, which the markets appreciate.

Handling Objections

The only thing ever stopping you from getting a sale is an objection you have not overcome. Think about it: if you can overcome *every* objection, you must get the sale, as long as you ask for it, of course. The question is: How?

No matter what product or service you are selling, or to whom you are selling, prospects are always going to raise objections to buying whatever you are selling. The trap many salespeople fall into is that they become offended or upset by these objections rather than seeing them as another avenue to get back to the sales presentation. Look at objections as opportunities. To help you with this, train yourself to be ready for any and all objections by preparing clear, logical answers in advance. Spend the necessary time to think about all the possible objections you might face, write them down, and decide how you will answer each and every concern a potential buyer might raise.

Recognizing Buying Signals

Let me tell you a story about Chuck Wollmer, one of my first franchisees in Miami, Florida. Part of my role and responsibility as a franchisor was to help franchisees with sales training. Chuck called me one day and said he had his first appointment with a twenty-five-employee restaurant, which was an ideal-size company for Paychex, so I decided to make a trip to Florida and go on the sales call with him.

We went to the restaurant and sat in one of the booths; the restaurant was closed so it was just us. Chuck went through the presentation, and there was no question he knew and understood our product, its features, its advantages and benefits in finite detail.

When we left the restaurant and were walking back to his car, he said, "That went well, didn't it?" My reply was that it was one of the worst sales presentations I'd ever witnessed. He was shocked, so I explained that he had failed to ask for the order, even though the owner had given him several strong buying signals. Chuck had been so wrapped up in his presentation he hadn't heard, or noticed, that the owner wanted to sign on the dotted line. The restaurant owner had said, "What do I do to get started?" and "When could we start?" Chuck, however, single-mindedly carried on with his presentation.

In any sales situation you need to listen to your prospect, really listen. There comes a point when prospects have enough information to make a decision and will ask you questions that indicate they are ready to commit to the purchase. These are the buying signals; learn to recognize them and when you do, move toward asking for the order.

On some occasions a prospect may become silent; do not take this as a negative. They may be thinking of all the reasons they should buy. Let the silence go on for however long it takes, and you will be rewarded with an order.

Chuck learned his lesson and went on to run a highly successful franchise and later became a key member of the Paychex management team.

Using Trial Closes

Trial closes are almost the reverse of buying signals. Whereas buying signals are initiated by the prospect, you the salesperson can ask questions to "test the waters" to see if a buyer is close to making a decision. For example, you might say, "We could start this service next week if you like," or "We could deliver your order the week after next. Will that work for you?"

If you use a trial close at a moment in the presentation when the buyer has all the information he or she needs, it can actually be a form of asking for the order or closing the sale. If the buyer is not ready, a trial close question will encourage the person to raise any remaining objections he or she might have about your product. At that point you can answer the questions and use a trial close a second or third time.

I remember once using a trial close and getting an extreme buying signal. I was selling to a printing firm, a father-and-son operation. I was making my sales presentation to the father, who was in his seventies. Their company had a twenty-person payroll, which was a great size for Paychex. The presentation went well, and I decided to employ a trial close: "Maybe we should start this next week. It'll give us time to get your payroll information together." I was surprised when he answered, "Can't you do it sooner than that? I might not live that long." Here was a case where the trial close led directly to the close as I replied, "Well, let's do it right now."

Often salespeople make closing far harder than it needs to be; sometimes you simply have to ask for the order.

Successful selling has three basic elements: identify a prospect that needs what you are selling; determine that the prospect has the power to make the buying decision; and ascertain that the prospect can afford or is willing to pay the price you need to charge to make a profit.

Understanding Your Competition

Some entrepreneurs and business moguls (and politicians—they're the worst) take an almost insane delight in dragging their competition and opponents through the mud. I never thought that was necessary. In fact, I think only losers take that approach.

I made it Paychex policy that no one in the company should ever disparage our competition. Competition keeps a company on its toes, and it also provides opportunity, so why not embrace it? My strategy was always to *compliment* my competition. People don't expect that, and once again, I think there is a benefit to doing things differently. I find my competitors provide a wealth (in more ways than one) of useful information.

The big advantage you can have over your competition, especially when starting out in business, is that you know what you are up against and can take action to position your product or service more favorably in terms of features, advantages, and benefits. For instance, you can set your price a little lower, knowing it will be harder for them to adjust their pricing in the short-term.

When I launched Paychex, I noticed ADP's fairly high minimum charges, so we came in at a much lower price point. We hurt them for quite a while before they could start matching our pricing. However, be careful, because lower prices don't always work, especially if the cost benefit doesn't outweigh the inconvenience of changing suppliers.

Salespeople and Your Competition

Your salesperson's primary responsibility is to convince prospects that what you offer is a better deal than what your competitors can offer. He or she needs to do this in an honest and ethical manner. Prospects make their buying decisions by weighing a great many factors, including the benefits of your product in comparison to others on offer, price, ability to deliver, reliability, and security, and whether they have faith in your company. Add to this personal biases, such as whether they like and trust the salesperson, and you can see that the road to an order is paved with tripping points. One such stumbling block for your salespeople is disparaging your competition. Most potential customers will take a dim view of your company if your salespeople openly criticize the competition. This strategy of integrity first will put your salespeople into a stronger position when dealing with prospects.

Competition exists in almost any enterprise that has ever been created, but rather than see competition constantly as a threat, look at the significant value competitors can bring to your company. What do I mean by this? Having competition helps you, maybe even forces you, to keep your product line viable and more desirable to your target market.

Competition also helps build an esprit de corps in your company, but you have to be careful this is achieved with integrity. You need to set a high standard of morality for your employees, one that makes it a policy not to disparage the company's competition. Do this, and your employees will respect you and be even stronger team players—they will be proud to work for your company.

When I was on the road selling, if I commented on our main competitor, ADP, it was to say that they were the leader in large company payroll processing and we were the leader in small business payroll processing. I would go on to say that without the pioneering work carried out by ADP, Paychex wouldn't even exist. This kind of approach will sit well with both potential customers and your salespeople.

I mentioned earlier that competition keeps your products viable and desirable; I should add "current" to that list. Some years ago, Paychex introduced a product called Taxpay directly as a result of watching the success ADP had with a similar product. Without getting into the technical and fiduciary details, this product, or it might better be referred to as a service, determines the taxes due on a client's payroll and allows Paychex to pay the amount to the IRS using the client's own funds. This takes a great deal of responsibility and work away from small businesses. It is a convenient and trouble-free service that is extremely popular. I have to confess that initially I didn't think small business owners would allow us to take money out of their accounts because they would be concerned about their cash flow. In this case I was wrong.

Once we decided to introduce Taxpay, it took us about a year to catch up with ADP's success with this product, during which time they were eating our lunch in no uncertain terms. However, as I write this, 95 percent of our new clients sign up for this service, and it is a profitable part of Paychex's product line.

In my defense, ADP also adopted one of our services, payroll tax returns, that we had offered from the day the company launched. As with our adoption of Taxpay, it took them quite some time to realize the benefit of offering this service.

The lesson here is to keep a very close eye on your competition. Are they offering potential customers anything more, or better, than your salespeople have in their bag? Your sales manager should create a feedback loop with all members of his or her sales force so that any information relating to the strengths and weaknesses of your competition is duly noted, and then you can compare their strengths and weaknesses to your own. Once you have the results of that analysis, you can ensure their weaknesses become your strengths, while at the same time matching them strength for strength.

Respecting your competition and learning from them when they do something better than you is a sound strategy. Competition is good; good competition is better, as long as you watch the companies concerned carefully and keep one step ahead.

Hiring Salespeople

The most difficult people to hire are often salespeople. First, it's extremely hard to find people who are good at selling. Second, the whole issue of compensation—salary, salary plus commission, or commission only—can be a minefield. However, Paychex has had thousands of excellent salespeople work for the company over the years, so I can assure you they are out there.

Some would say hiring salespeople is like going to Las Vegas: it's a gamble. You can do a lot of interviewing, you can check a lot of references, but in some cases, despite all of this, you're not going to be successful in hiring the right person. Let me give you some advice based on my experience of hiring hundreds of salespeople in the constant search for those who can actually sell and reach sales quotas.

First, if someone has prior sales experience, that's a good start. It doesn't mean they are any good, but at least you are on the right track. You can and should check with their previous employer or employers, and ask how successful they were, or ask the candidate whether they have any awards, letters, internal emails, or trade press coverage to show how successful they have been. If their employer is noncommittal and has nothing that validates their claim of being a top producer, you might want to tread carefully.

I've found that the best salespeople are those who have played sports at a competitive level and experienced a degree of success. It shows they are used to working hard and that they are highly competitive; that's what you want to see in a salesperson.

I was constantly on the lookout for good salespeople when I was running Paychex. For example, one winter day my car was sliding down a hill, so I pulled into a tire store, conveniently located at the bottom of the hill, to buy some better winter tires. A pleasant young man looked after me. His level of service and his attitude were great, so I asked him if he would ever consider a sales job. He said sure, so I got him an interview. Within three or four years, he was one of the top five salespeople in the company. I'll talk about hiring for attitude and then giving that person all the training he or she needs in chapter 6.

Recruiting Competitors' Salespeople

This is something I outlawed at Paychex. We never tried to encourage good salespeople to leave the competitor they were working for and join Paychex. I never felt it was a fair way to do business. It takes a lot of time and money to train salespeople, and then even more time for them to become comfortable and skilled at selling your product.

I've often been asked by entrepreneurs how they can ensure their best salespeople are not stolen away by competitors. The best way is to make it clear that your company will not indulge in the practice of poaching good people. Set an example, and hopefully you will gain the respect of your competitors. Another thing I have done in the past is call competitors' CEOs and openly discuss the issue with them. If you can get an agreement that neither of you will actively engage in poaching, it can go a long way to preventing such activity.

Managing a Sales Force

To protect your own people from being lured away, ensure your sales team is happy, well paid, well trained, respected, and made to feel they are part of the bigger picture and the future of the company. People can only be recruited by one of your competitors if they are willing to leave.

I'm not going to give you a complete management lesson here— this is not an MBA course—but I do want to highlight a few things I've always found that made it more likely the salespeople working for me were both content and highly productive.

Whether you are just starting a company, own a going concern, or manage a sales force, there are certain keys to building a successful, motivated, and committed sales team.

The first is the compensation plan, which has to have a balance between incentive and base pay. For example, if a compensation plan is too heavily oriented toward base salary and too low on the incentive or commission side, salespeople may not be encouraged to work as hard as someone with a higher incentive component. In my experience, something in the fifty-fifty range seems to work best for most people.

Although it's not necessarily an entrepreneur's first thought, expenses and their payment can be part of the compensation plan, though this is an area full of potential problems. Expense reports can make liars out of honest people; there is too much room for misrepresentation. Administratively, expense reports are also a big hassle for salespeople and companies. Each expense has to be itemized, receipts provided, and someone in the company has to make a value judgment as to whether each line is reasonable and legitimate and then approve or disapprove the claim.

From the very beginning of Paychex, I instigated a no-nonsense expense system for salespeople. We decided on a fair, flat-dollar amount per pay period that sales staff would receive to cover their expenses. This removed any necessity of providing expense receipts or completing and submitting expense reports to management.

Doing this also means it's up to the individual salesperson to justify to the IRS what their actual expenses were versus the reimbursement they were given. Salespeople are therefore less likely to exaggerate their expenses, and this approach also removes the challenge of monitoring them, while simplifying the whole reimbursement of expenses for your accounting department.

Activity Reports and Sales Quotas

I would encourage you to have your salespeople fill out some sort of activity report. Whether it's once a week or once a month, an activity report allows you to monitor the number of presentations they are making and how many prospects they are closing, and to decide if these are acceptable rates of productivity and success. Without activity reports you will have little idea how individuals are performing, how your overall sales team is performing, and whether you are meeting your company's revenue targets.

I'd like to share a sales and management strategy we introduced at Paychex after the company went from being a disparate group of individual businesses to a single corporate entity (the process I referred to earlier as consolidation) and we reorganized our entire operation.

In a nutshell, the new management structure allowed for each zone manager to oversee eight sales managers who in turn directed the efforts of eight salespeople. When a region grew and required more than eight salespeople, a new sales manager would be hired. Subsequently, when a zone grew to have more than eight sales managers, territories would be redistributed, a new zone would be created, and a new zone manager hired. This eight-to-one system worked well for us during a period where we enjoyed consistent growth.

With a new structure in the sales organization, it was important to have appropriate sales quotas. The numbers needed to make sense based on historical reality. If you can justify how you arrived at objective sales targets, it's far harder for people to question them or claim they are too high. Initially we came up with what we expected for the company as a whole, then through discussions with the zone managers and sales managers we looked at each territory one by one to come up with fair, attainable quotas. This buy-in was important to prevent any resentment among zones.

Once we had the overall sales targets by region, we broke these down even further to provide weekly quotas for each sales rep. They would be expected to submit a weekly activity report to company headquarters. Back then I reviewed these reports myself. My expectation for salespeople was that they did at least forty cold calls a week, leading to a minimum of eight face-to-face presentations, of which they were expected to close no less than two new clients.

The key to this strategy was that I could compare reports sales rep to sales rep and zone to zone. Having that depth of information allowed me and other senior managers to understand what was going on out in the field and take immediate action, when and if necessary.

The simple fact that we were collecting this information added to the level of accountability all parties felt; it also gave us credibility when we needed to confront any issues in the field.

Training Salespeople

Training salespeople is paramount. They have to have the ability to make presentations to potential customers, in a way the customer understands, that show the features, advantages, and benefits of the product. They have to be confident enough in what they are selling to handle objections and close sales.

Ongoing sales training has been a major factor in Paychex's success, and I can't emphasize enough that you should make it an integral part of your overall sales strategy. Bringing together your sales team at least once a year for a sales conference and sales training, where you update them on your company's goals and vision, will motivate them and ensure they are recommitted to your company when they return to their territories. They will also have the opportunity to share success stories, along with any challenges they face, with their colleagues.

Ensuring your salespeople are completely familiar with the products they are selling is important. Knowing a product intimately when talking about it, or demonstrating it, boosts confidence in both the salesperson and the prospect.

———

I'll close this chapter with a story about making a sale that one of my partners, Jack Hartland, quickly regretted. In the next chapter, I'll tell you more about the strange way Jack ended up becoming my partner.

One day during his training, he came into the Rochester office in a state of great excitement. He said, "I sold a fifty-person payroll!" He handed one of our staff the employees' personal payroll information. About fifteen minutes later she came into my office and exclaimed, "Tom, you're not going to believe this. This trucking company Jack just brought in—every mobster in the city is on the payroll!" I called Jack and told him he'd better ensure when he delivered their first payroll it was 100 percent accurate! We ended up handling that account for several years, but not without some trepidation. It's a competitive world out there and a sale is a sale, although I think Jack had mixed views about that trucking company.

My final advice? Close early and close often.

Takeaways

- Cash flow problems are a direct result of not generating enough revenue through sales. Therefore, they are actually a sales problem, not a cash flow problem.
- Nothing happens in a company until somebody sells something.
- The biggest mistake entrepreneurs make is a tendency to overestimate their ability to sell their product or service.
- The best person to sell your product initially is you.
- It is imperative to know the status of sales against forecasts at all times.
- Beware sleeping with elephants—that is, relying heavily on any major client that accounts for a sizeable percentage of overall sales revenue.

- All customers are not of equal value; sometimes there can be greater profit in smaller accounts. Diversity in customer sizes offers predictability and safety.
- The only thing preventing a sale is an objection; overcome every objection and you will get the sale.
- Recognizing buying signals and acting on them leads to more sales.
- Using trial closes makes asking for the order easier and more effective.
- Never disparage the competition; competitors keep your company competitive.
- Carrying out a comprehensive strengths and weaknesses analysis of both your company and your competitors will reveal sales and marketing opportunities.
- Make your competitors' weaknesses your strengths.
- Instigate no-nonsense activity reports, sales quotas, compensation plans, and expense reporting.
- Always be on the lookout for good salespeople.
- Train salespeople well so they know the product intimately.
- The key to good cash flow? Close early and close often.

SIX

HIRE FOR ATTITUDE, TRAIN FOR SKILL, FIRE WHEN NECESSARY

I was certainly not handed success on a silver platter. I did not inherit money to invest or take over a thriving family business I could grow to the next level. Everything I have achieved I built from scratch through hard work and enterprise, and often out of sheer necessity. More importantly, I didn't do it alone. I learned very early in my business career the importance of treating people well—of showing them respect and encouraging their cooperation.

However, you have to be prepared to deal with people who have unrealistic expectations about how they might be compensated. I remember when we took Paychex public, we had a party; the management team at that time consisted of seventeen men. Afterward, one of the guys said, "Tom, could we get something to signify our entry into this thing?" I asked him what he was thinking, and he said, "Well, like a founder's ring." Another asked whether they could all have their portraits in the boardroom. I was floored. I'd started the company in 1971 and these guys hadn't come on board until 1976, and they wanted a founder's ring? Right then I made some decisions on who was staying and who was going.

We are all a product of what happens to us, and much depends on how we react to those moments when a life lesson is presented to us. One such experience occurred when I was almost seventeen years old. It was summer, so there was no school, and my father was trying to recover from the collapse of his own business. He had taken a job as a truck driver, delivering macaroni products. I went with him most days during the summer break to keep him company and help carry boxes into the stores.

I remember feeling uncomfortable about the work my father was doing. My father was Sicilian, and his family had run many food businesses. The company he was working for was also run by Sicilian immigrants, so one would have expected a certain level of simpatico between the owners and management and my father, especially since they had all emigrated from the same place and worked in the same type of business. Unfortunately, that was not the case.

I can't remember exactly what caused the scene, but something had gone wrong in the warehouse and the manager laid into my father with a vengeance. He screamed at my father, "You are an incompetent, inefficient idiot." I was stunned. I could feel my father's humiliation radiating from him as I stood there silent, confused, embarrassed, and disgusted on his behalf. I didn't know what to do, so I didn't do anything. Neither did my father; he just took the tirade, and when it was over, he walked back to his truck and we drove off. The cab was silent, both of us keeping our thoughts to ourselves.

As I sat contemplating what had happened, I could feel my father's excruciating pain balanced by stoic resignation. There was nothing he could do; he desperately needed the job, and his superior held all the power. I made two decisions that day. The first was that I would do everything in my power never to work for someone else, and the second was that if I was ever in a position of authority over people, I would never treat an employee so disrespectfully—ever.

My HR Philosophy

I relate the story of my father's dressing down because that event was foundational to my HR philosophy and my overall business belief of bringing everyone along with me and creating a good deal for everyone.

Working alongside my father that day made me question the balance of power and the responsibility of the person holding the power to wield it with integrity, fairness, and compassion. That experience was instrumental in forming my opinions on respect, leadership, empowerment, and organizational culture. A leader's number one responsibility is to create a vision of growth and success, a vision for the following year's achievement level, and to empower his or her employees to do the same. That's what I always considered to be the most important part of my job.

I was always committed to my HR philosophy, but I can't say I was the best person to deal with day-to-day HR issues. As an entrepreneur or manager, you don't have to do or be good at everything. Delegation is a good leadership skill.

My best friend, Gene Polisseni, was a huge asset to Paychex. He was responsible for creating the sales organization and later formed the HR, training, and telemarketing departments. As I mentioned, he was also responsible for starting our 401(k) services, which today account for a significant portion of Paychex's revenue.

I could see his office from mine; people would continually walk past my door to visit him. He was the company counselor; people warmed to him, and he gave good advice. He'd listen. I didn't have the patience for that kind of stuff; I thought of Gene as the soul of the company.

It's important to have someone who can take care of personnel issues. You can't run a business without dealing with the challenges your employees face, both personally and while at work.

At the end of the day, the best way to treat employees is to go by the Golden Rule: do unto others as you would have them do unto you.

Corporate Culture and the Growing Company

The thing with corporate culture is that either you have one by default, or you create one that fits with your philosophy and values. I would wholeheartedly suggest you do the latter.

In the very early days of Paychex, the company acted like a fraternity. My partners and franchisees were, for the most part, inexperienced in business and lacked the entrepreneurial qualities that would normally have been a prerequisite for starting a business. For example, our disparate group included a doorman from the Boca Raton Hotel and Club and two car salesmen.

Changing the corporate culture, therefore, was not without its challenges. One such area of conflict with my partners and employees was our annual sales conferences, which were held at exotic locations such as Hawaii, Arizona, Atlanta, or Disney World. Every year I'd get asked, "Why can't we bring our spouses?" The argument given by those privileged to attend was that their spouses were part of their success. My counterargument was that to stay on budget, we'd have to halve the number of salespeople attending if we allowed spouses to attend. Not only that, where did the definition of spouse stop? Life partner, significant other, any plus one?

I also pointed out that the one year we did allow spouses to attend a lot of cliques formed, which was the opposite of what we were trying to achieve. That was really the heart of the matter. The conferences were about the sales team sharing ideas. The concept of it being work, albeit in a nice location, was lost on most of those attending.

The other issue against allowing spouses at these types of work events was that inevitably some overbearing or overly ambitious spouse would have the temerity to confront management demanding better terms or treatment for a significant other.

There was one further consideration, of course, and that was that conferences could be a little on the wild side. Most salespeople were between the ages of twenty-five and thirty-five, and they were away from home and letting their hair down. We had several occasions where somebody drank too much and harassed a colleague; I always felt the potential for disruption would escalate if spouses were in attendance.

This was partly the reason I began limiting alcohol at corporate functions. I still believe it has no place in a work environment, even when that work environment has a social aspect. It was, however, only part of the reason, because there was another catalyst for my change in attitude toward alcohol.

On the day we took Paychex public I attended the funeral of Gene's daughter, who was the victim of a DWI car crash. She was a passenger in the car and was so badly injured that her parents were unable to say their last goodbyes; they were forced to have a closed-casket funeral. Both her father and I quit drinking alcohol that day, and to this day I think it serves no purpose. Especially in a business environment.

Forcing People to Donate

One event early in my career had a big impact on the corporate culture I built at Paychex and ultimately the respect we had, and still have, for employees. It occurred in my late teens when I was a bank teller.

I was checking my weekly paycheck and found a form outlining the bank's support of the United Way Community Chest. It asked me to authorize the bank to deduct a minimum of 50 cents a week from my salary. At the time I thought little of it. I hadn't heard of the

Community Chest and was not about to support a cause I didn't know. After all, I was also a good cause—my education was important—so I threw the form away.

Shortly after, my boss approached me to ask why he hadn't received my authorization form. I explained my situation and that I had decided at this time it was more important for me to save for my education. I was polite and felt my reasoned explanation would suffice. It was then I learned a valuable lesson about how companies sometimes pressure employees to support causes that will bring the firm credibility and publicity.

The vice president of HR summoned me to his office. He told me that the bank expected all employees to contribute to the United Way campaign. I repeated my position and was told that if I didn't comply, it would go on my permanent record. I remember feeling threatened by someone who should have had my best interests at heart. My heart was pounding, and it felt as though I was back again standing beside my father in the macaroni warehouse.

I promised myself that day that I would never demand any of my employees donate to a charitable organization, let alone threaten them, no matter how good the cause or how important participation was to the company or its image.

Since that day I have given over one-quarter of a billion dollars to charitable causes. I'll go out on a limb and say I've more than made up for not donating fifty cents a week to the United Way while working for little more than minimum wage.

Respect Goes Both Ways

I wholeheartedly believe that senior management should show employees respect, but I've always felt it's a two-way street. One of the things that always annoyed me at Paychex was when I walked through the offices after everyone had gone home and found messy, cluttered desks.

Maybe twice a year I would walk around a random department after hours and find a desk that was particularly messy. I'd throw everything on the desk into a waste basket. It didn't take long the next morning for word to get around that I was always watching. I expected desks to be free of clutter when people left for the day. I realize this may make me sound like a control (or maybe clean) freak, but it was important to me and I felt it was important to our corporate brand. We processed our customers' payrolls, so precision was fundamental to everything we did. I wanted to demonstrate that order and precision should be top of mind at every level throughout the company.

As I've explained, I believe that establishing a positive, well-defined organizational culture is important. However, lack of growth can stifle creative thinking and encourage an overtly political atmosphere. Balance is key.

Hiring the Right People

Hiring and firing effectively is central to a good HR policy. The second employee I ever hired at Paychex is still with the company some forty-five years later. *That's* a good hire!

I always worked on the general basis of hiring for attitude, training for skill. This may not be an original thought, but hey, if it isn't broken, don't fix it. Over the years I have developed several interview techniques, including testing, that help me identify the good from the not so good and the indifferent.

Being selective is one of the keys to good hiring. There is a cost to educating and training a new hire, not to mention a transition period where the person is not performing to full capacity. This is especially true of salespeople. I've always believed in building a quality workforce through skillful and careful hiring and through superior training.

As I mentioned previously, I've always been drawn to hiring people who played competitive team sports. There is something about people who like to win in a team environment that often makes them good employees. Ambition and perseverance are also attractive qualities in candidates.

I promised earlier to tell you the story of Jack Hartland. Jack wanted to be my partner some fifty years ago, and the more I tried to turn him away, the more determined he was to join Paychex. He worked for Pontiac, a division of General Motors, as a district manager, but he wasn't happy. I got a telephone call one day from his brother-in-law, who told me they'd heard about our partnerships and franchises and said he and Jack would like to meet with me. I told them I only partnered with people I knew well. He pushed, and rather than be impolite, I agreed to a meeting at a restaurant, where we had lunch and talked about Paychex. They asked lots of questions, which I answered while making it as clear as I could that I was not going to partner with Jack, as I knew nothing about him. Unperturbed, Jack got up from the table, went out to his car, and brought back a wallet. He opened it up and an accordion-style series of pockets flipped out, displaying a dozen or so photographs. He said, "This is my wife, these are my kids, my dog, my house." I looked at him with as much compassion as I could muster and said, "Jack, so what? I'm just not interested."

I returned to my office and forgot all about Jack Hartland. A month later one of my staff came into my office and said, "There's a Jack Hartland on the phone for you." I remember thinking, *That name sounds familiar, but I can't quite place it.* I picked up the phone and the voice on the other end said, "Tom, I'm ready. I've sold my house. I quit my job. I want to move to Houston." I responded, "What?"

I asked him to give me a few more details and then told him to hang on. I put him on hold while I gathered my senses. What could I do? The poor guy had done all this just to become part of Paychex, so I said to myself, "What the heck?" I got back on the line and told him, "Be here for training starting in two weeks." He did all right at Paychex and was a good sales guy.

There are other times you have to fight, well, almost, to bring someone on board who you believe will be a great asset to the company. Such was the case with Bob Sebo. He worked around the corner from my office as a district manager for General Motors' Cadillac division, and we often met for coffee. He and I used to play euchre, a card game, regularly with my friends Gene and Gary.

Bob became interested in the concept of what I'd referred to as "recurring revenue" and what he called "residual income." He liked that in the payroll business, you sold a customer once, and if you looked after their interests you could earn revenue from them the next year and the next. Unlike in the car business, where you had to resell a customer a new car every few years. He was correct, of course, that this was a more lucrative business model.

It was a long time ago and we were both young, so I wasn't surprised when he asked me to meet his parents to help convince them it was a good idea for him to leave what they considered an excellent job at Cadillac to join what was still little more than a start-up. Bob's dad was only about five five, but he was a tough, feisty guy. Bob told him he was leaving GM to come work with me, and I remember his father saying, "Are you frickin' nuts?!" Then he looked at me and said, "I oughta kick your ass, and his too!"

I thought he was going to get up from his chair and deliver on his promise, but he calmed down and it all worked out well. Bob's father ended up working in the business delivering payrolls; his mother took computer classes in her late seventies and became a payroll specialist for several years. Years later Bob's father told him, "I sure almost made you make the wrong decision, didn't I?"

Bob once said to me he hoped back then to become a "thousand-aire." Well, he ended up being a whole lot more than that. By way of an epilogue, Paychex still has some of Bob's clients in his Cleveland office who have been with the company for more than forty years.

Interview Techniques

There have been hundreds of thousands of words written about how to interview job applicants, and I'm not going to repeat them here; what I will do is tell you how I handle interviews, or at least the key things I want to know and the techniques I use to discover whether someone is going to be good for the company. Interviewing can be simple. Keeping to the basics is often the best way to approach this important growth-oriented endeavor.

As I mentioned earlier, I look for people with ambition, people who have energy, people who want to win. If they want to win for themselves, they are going to want to win for the company.

I want a job applicant to have done their homework and to know a lot about my company; if they haven't bothered to do their research, then why should I bother to give them my time? I also want to know why they left their last job or jobs. The answer to that question can raise a lot of concerns, or alternatively indicate I'm sitting opposite a future employee. For instance, they may start complaining about their former company or bashing management. Or they may start into a long-winded story. These are huge red flags. If they are reticent or unwilling to supply a reference for their most recent employer or any key employer, that is a major concern, as are obvious blanks in their résumé.

Want to know my most effective interview technique? Silence. Let the interviewee talk and when they stop, don't say a word. What they say next may turn the whole interview into negative or positive territory, or they may simply wait for you to speak. Is there a correct way for them to treat the pause? I think the best thing they can do is let the silence hang. The interviewer may just be thinking or considering his or her next question or, like me, they could just be testing the person! The pregnant pause is a most effective tool in any interview.

Another technique I use is to listen and watch how they handle themselves throughout the interview process. I really believe the saying "Hire for attitude, train for skill." It's a lot easier to train someone to do a particular job than to change their poor attitude or manners. During an interview I will offer water or coffee to the candidate, which one of my assistants will bring them. I am looking to see if they display common courtesy by saying thank you to the person handing them their beverage. After the interview I watch to see if they leave the glass or cup on the table for someone else to clear away. Finally, do they push their chair back into place? To me, these few gestures of basic civility and respect tell me a lot about a person.

Finally, you have to question the validity of their references. HR departments have been trained to lie, or at least obfuscate the truth. Legally they have to be careful about what information they provide to you regarding an ex-employee, but there is a simple question they *can* answer and that is, "Would you rehire this person?" You could perhaps make that question more pointed by rephrasing it as, "Is this person eligible for rehire?" Asking one of those questions and listening carefully, not only to the answer but to the way it is delivered, may well tell you what you need to know.

The number one question you should ask yourself when hiring is, "Can this person help us grow?" The answer to that will be a deciding factor on whether to hire a candidate or move on to the next prospect.

Testing

Over the years at Paychex we used various types of personality testing to assist in either hiring or promoting senior management people. Used wisely these can be a useful tool for HR departments. I remember on one occasion all senior management took such a test, including me, and I thought the guy handling the analysis had done a good job. Until, that is, I read his report on me, in which he said I had a tendency to have an occasional emotional reaction to an issue. A few days later I saw him walking past my office and called him in for a chat. I told him that I didn't think the description was accurate and that I was almost always calm and collected in my dealings with people.

He reviewed my file and said that there was no sign of this behavior during the interview portion of the test, but that it had come out of the written questionnaire. He then looked at me and out of the blue said, "Do you eat a lot of chocolate?" I was amazed, because I am known for my love of chocolate, but he would not have known this. It turns out that chocolate contains phenethylamine, a molecule that resembles amphetamine and some other psychoactive stimulants, so it can potentially be mood altering if you eat enough.

My point is that the more you can do to understand people prior to hiring them, the better, especially if they might turn out to be a chocoholic.

Nepotism Notes

Hiring family members can be a risky strategy, primarily because it's tough to fire them. I knew a car dealer who owned multiple dealerships that he ran with his daughter. They worked well together . . . until she got married and brought her husband into the business. Her father loved his son-in-law, and the young man was doing great in the business. Sometime later, the father sold the business to his son-in-law and even helped him with the financing. Unfortunately, when his daughter's marriage ended, the whole business arrangement blew up in their faces. The lawyers were the only ones left smiling when it eventually got sorted out.

While I was at Paychex, I imposed a policy forbidding nepotism, which was extremely unpopular. Let me explain in more detail why rules around nepotism are so important for the effective running of any company. For example, if you have a supervisor who hires her nephew and is later unhappy with the job he is doing, what can she do about it? She is in an extremely difficult, if not untenable, situation. Not only does the supervisor's relationship with the nephew become precarious, but her relationship with her own brother or sister may be affected as well. The company also suffers. If the supervisor doesn't handle the situation delicately, one of two things happens: if she lets the poor performance slide, productivity suffers; if she has the courage to fire him, productivity suffers during the rehiring process. Nepotism usually doesn't pay off for companies.

Employment Contracts

I suggest you use employment contracts for two main reasons. First, they are important, even for small companies, if you are to minimize the risk of employees leaving and competing against you, stealing your clients, or poaching your employees.

Second, and this is especially true when dealing with senior management employees, it ensures that both you and your employee fully understand how compensation is to be paid. If there are bonus situations or incentive contracts of any kind, the details of those need to be fully disclosed and understood by both parties.

A word of warning here: different states have differing ideas of what an employment contract is and its enforceability. Be careful to investigate the rules, regulations, and laws surrounding employment contracts in your jurisdiction prior to drawing up your contracts.

Fringe Benefits

To employers, fringe benefits can be like a graduated income tax; they usually start out small, but over time they can grow significantly and become a large cost. I would caution any entrepreneur to be conservative when starting new fringe benefits, such as a 401(k) plan, and grow into them slowly.

Eastman Kodak, which no longer exists in the form it used to, had a very liberal pension plan, which eventually they could no longer afford to finance. This presented the company with a significant balance sheet problem.

Employers can operate 401(k) plans in two ways. One is where only employees contribute and contributions are taken from their paychecks. The other option is that employers can match some of the employee's payments. My advice here is to be careful you don't start something you will later regret or not be able to afford to maintain.

Providing health insurance is almost mandatory today. My suggestion, if you are a start-up or a fairly new company, is that you only pay for individual employees themselves. If they have a family, let them pay that portion. It's a good way to get started, with one proviso: if your competition is offering better benefits, you may have to be more generous to remain competitive and attract well-qualified and desirable job candidates.

The Importance of Training

I have strong feelings not only about the necessity for high-caliber training but also about treating trainees well while they are undertaking training, especially when they're away from home. This philosophy stems from how I was treated when I was a twenty-four-year-old sales rep working for Burroughs Corporation selling accounting machines. The company flew me and several others to Detroit for five weeks of training; we were not allowed to drive our own cars.

When I arrived, I discovered that my fellow trainees and I would be staying at a converted YMCA in a dismal and scary part of town. It was the sort of area where it was wise not to walk around alone. My room was tiny, about eight feet by eight feet, with a small bed, a dresser, and a bathroom down the hall. It was similar to living in barracks, and at 6:30 a.m., like reveille, a bell would ring to wake us up and a school bus would pick us up an hour later. It felt like prison transportation. It was midsummer, and the bus had no air-conditioning.

We'd arrive every morning at a factory building, which was okay compared to the dormitory, and breakfast, lunch, and dinner were provided. We'd work all day and then be transported back to the hostel. This went on for five weeks. To me it reflected very negatively on the company.

Without vehicles, my fellow trainees and I, all guys in our mid-twenties, were trapped in the wrong part of town with no access to anywhere we could get some rest and relaxation. After three weeks I'd had enough. I broke the rules and went back to Rochester for the weekend and then drove back in my car. This, of course, made me somewhat of a hero and very popular.

It was another defining moment for me. I decided that if I was ever responsible for a sales force, I would deal with my salespeople very differently. They would be housed in good hotels, given decent meals and transportation, and treated with respect.

How did this affect my overall approach to training? Six years after Paychex went public, we'd outgrown our head office facility. The offices we had built in 1983 were no longer meeting our needs. Our revenues had reached a staggering $101 million, and our growth rate over the previous nine years was between 20 and 25 percent; by the end of 1989 we had more than 100,000 clients. We made the decision to build a 107,000-square-foot addition onto our existing building, tripling its size.

The extensive amount of training we gave our employees was already at that time a key component of our success. It was one of the differentiators between us and our competition. The new extension allowed us to demonstrate that further. Our architect suggested that we place the training department in the main lobby so that when visitors arrived, they would be surrounded by classrooms.

This was revolutionary thinking at the time; training departments were normally stuck in basements or located off-site. The thought of visitors witnessing firsthand the importance of training excited me. Thousands of people visited our head office every year to learn about our products and services and attend sales training and other courses. The idea of showcasing training at our head office demonstrated to sales trainees and others how important they were to the company and the value we placed on their performance and contribution to the company.

Once the new addition opened, I'd walk into the building and wave to the trainees; it established a connection with them, and sometimes I'd chat with them in the corridors or even in the dining room. It was a marvelous leveler; they felt they were an integral part of the company and that we valued them—which of course we did. After all, they were the ones on the front line bringing in new clients every day. When they returned to their branches across the country, they talked about their time at corporate headquarters and had pride in being part of something bigger.

An added bonus is that Wall Street analysts take notice and are impressed. Today, Paychex delivers over a million hours of training (over 305,000 of those hours are instructor led) to its more than 15,500 employees.

Training remains at the heart of Paychex; today, if you walk into the impressive circular lobby of the company's headquarters, you will stand at the reception desk and still be encircled by training rooms. Training is the core of our business, and that becomes obvious to every single visitor. And the people in those training rooms also know they are extremely important to the success of the business.

Training Fun

The new training center was also responsible for a great deal of in-house entertainment, some of which was at my expense. Trainees and management would prank me on occasion, and I managed to turn the tables on them a few times too.

Running a public company, it turned out, wasn't just about numbers. One thing I was known for was keeping things clean and tidy, and trainees knew they would be in trouble if they left a coffee cup, trash, or food in a training room when they left for the day. (You might recall my story about emptying the contents of a messy desk into the trash.)

With that in mind, let me tell you the story of when the HR department pranked me—and good. We used to hold graduation day lunches. These were formal affairs; everyone was expected to wear business attire, and although celebratory, they were taken seriously.

During one such occasion, I was presenting Paychex's four-year plan. Just as I was getting into my stride outlining the business plan, a loud noise started up behind me. I turned around and there was a person wearing janitorial clothing vacuuming the back of the room. I couldn't believe it. I turned around and thundered, "What the heck is going on here? You can't do that now. Can't you see I'm making a presentation?" She looked puzzled and then brought out what looked like a work order and handed it to me. I gave it a cursory glance and said, "Forget it. Please leave!" The recruits were laughing, but I soon settled them down and got back to my presentation.

Later, the same woman started washing the outside of the room's glass windows, which was once again highly distracting. Now infuriated, I marched out of the room and shooed her unceremoniously away—again. As I did this, I looked across at the dining room where the entire HR department had gathered; they were all laughing their tails off, and I suddenly realized, red-faced, the whole thing had been staged.

On more than one occasion, however, I got back at them. As I mentioned, I would walk past the training department several times daily, and on one occasion I noticed that everyone in the management training class looked especially bored. I thought no more of it until a few nights later when I bumped into some of the middle managers at a local bar and we got talking. They were all from out of town and we had a stimulating conversation. One guy impressed me a lot, so I pulled him aside and said, "Do you want to have some fun?"

Graduation day for this group came around and we were at the luncheon. As usual, I was scheduled to address the new graduates. I was known for going off script a little at these affairs, and the training instructors and the head of the department were always nervous about what I might say. I could see they were relieved, however, when I didn't say anything controversial on this particular day. My address was followed by a Q&A session. That was when the fun started.

The manager, Chris, whom I'd met at the bar, stood up and complained, "I'm a little disappointed with our software when it comes to handling local income taxes." I answered, "Yes, Chris, I agree, it doesn't meet our standards, but we're working on it." I then looked around the room for questions from other people who'd raised their hands. Before anyone else could ask another question, however, Chris stood up again and said, "Tom, I'm not happy with your answer." The instructor now moved into a position next to this guy and was resting a hand on his arm in an attempt to settle him down, or perhaps warn him of imminent peril should he persist with this aggressive questioning and complaining.

By this time, I was showing my irritation and said curtly, "We're working on it. We're doing it as fast as we can." I answered a few more questions, and he stood up a third time and came at me hard. "I think your answer is bullshit." I could see the face of the head of the department—she was horrified. I took a moment, looked long and hard at Chris, and said, "Look, that's the way it is; if you don't like it, there's the door—use it!" At that, Chris stormed out.

My head of training's jaw fell open; it was graduation day and I'd just thrown out one of her best graduates. The room was silent and in shock after Chris walked out of the room. A moment later, however, Chris came back into the room with an ear-to-ear grin and everybody started laughing and applauding our performance. I'm not sure I endeared myself to the training managers that day, but the trainees sure appreciated it.

We had a lot of fun in those days, and our trainees always knew I had their backs. I remember once dropping into a sales conference to check on the quality of the material we were delivering. I'd hired an outside consultant to make a presentation and wanted to hear what he had to say. On this occasion we had about five hundred salespeople in attendance and they were all, as was I, waiting to gain some new knowledge. Unfortunately, his opening words were, "Telephone marketing is vital, and what you are selling is an easy pitch. I could get on the phone, and I bet you in an hour I could make two or three sales."

I knew that type of boast was not going to go down well with my highly professional and experienced salespeople, so I interrupted him and said I'd take him up on his bet. I went on, "I'll arrange for a phone to be brought in, so our salespeople can see firsthand how you make those sales." I've never seen a person fold so quickly; he actually ran out of the room.

My advice to you is to take training your employees seriously but have fun at the same time. Having a motivated, committed team in any department will repay any investment you might make in providing top-quality training.

This was one of my founding principles back in 1971, and as I write this, Paychex has recently been recognized as one of the Top 125 training organizations by *Training* magazine for the eighteenth consecutive year. In fact, it now holds twelfth place, jumping up eight spots since 2017. No wonder Paychex is one of the most respected payroll processing companies in the country.

Firing When Necessary

Firing someone is never fun, but on occasion it is entirely necessary. I believe in giving people more than one chance, so I have rarely if ever fired anyone for a single misdemeanor. Of course, employment law needs to be followed in all cases, and there are plenty of books and websites that will educate you as to your legal obligations and responsibilities. The biggest piece of advice I can give you is not to procrastinate and to always deal with personnel issues immediately. Call the person into your office and talk to them; get their side of the story, offer assistance to help them get back on track if applicable, and move on, leaving them with the clear knowledge that the next time you call them into your office, the conversation will go a little differently.

Negative Energy

I once had to reprimand one of my early partners who had become a regional manager after we consolidated the company. He was a nice guy and I liked him, but after a few drinks his behavior toward women became a problem, especially at sales conferences. He simply didn't understand boundaries, and he persistently harassed female employees. To compound the problem, he was married, not to mention that one of the women he hit on was my girlfriend, but that's another story—perhaps for my autobiography. I warned him several times and eventually had to call him into my office. I said, "You're a slow learner—you're fired."

There are many grounds for dismissal, from poor performance and bad behavior to criminal activity, but there is another occasion where you may need to get rid of someone whose attitude is causing a serious problem, and that is when they exude negative energy. When I owned the Buffalo Sabres, we had a player who fell into this category. The rest of the team didn't like him when he was on the ice (off the ice he was a nice guy), and he was affecting team morale. His work ethic was suspect, and on the ice he was an opportunist; he hung around the net waiting for a pass, so he could score and get all the glory. Although he was our top scorer, I traded him, and you know what? We won more games.

Negative energy can come down to something as simple as someone who constantly complains or whines about everything and nothing. I once had a senior manager who radiated negative energy; he was always complaining. On one occasion he came to me moaning about the number of intercorporate emails he received, telling me that most of them were unnecessary. I asked him to show me a few that were not important. Of course, he couldn't and left my office hopefully reconsidering his attitude.

Business owners and managers often ask me how they can prevent negative energy from taking hold in their company. I tell them that the number one thing they can do is to grow—growth feeds positive energy. During periods of growth, people are happier, politics is reduced to a minimum, and there is little time for backstabbing; people are just too busy. When you stop growing, however, people get stressed, they get competitive fighting over fewer opportunities, and things begin to deteriorate.

Takeaways

- It's important to treat people with respect and encourage cooperation.
- It makes good business sense to bring everyone along with you and create situations where it's a good deal for everyone.
- If you hold the balance of power, it is your responsibility to wield it with integrity, fairness, and compassion.
- The thing with corporate culture is that either you have one by default, or you create one that fits with your philosophy and values. The latter is preferable.

- Establishing a positive, well-defined organizational culture is important. However, if overdone it can stifle creative thinking and encourage an overtly political atmosphere and lead to backstabbing. Balance is key.
- Build a quality workforce through skillful and careful hiring and superior training.
- The pregnant pause is an effective tool in any interview.
- Negative energy damages businesses. Deal with it sooner rather than later.
- Hiring family members can be a risky strategy—it's tough to fire them.
- Be conservative when introducing new fringe benefits.
- Training should be at the center of any business.
- Take training your employees seriously but have fun at the same time. Having a motivated, committed team in any department will repay any investment you might make in providing top-quality training.

SEVEN

LEAD, FOLLOW, OR GET
OUT OF THE WAY

I used to have a double-sided sign on my desk at Paychex that said, on the side that faced visitors, "Lead, Follow, or Get Out of the Way," and on the reverse, "It's All in the Presentation." Occasionally I'd turn the sign around and show people my side. The phrase about leading or following has been used by many people, including Ted Turner, Lee Iacocca, and General George S. Patton, but that doesn't make it any less relevant when discussing leadership and management. No book on the principles of business success can ignore the importance of the person at its helm, whether that's for the whole company, a division, a department, or a branch.

In chapter 1, I discussed what I look for in an entrepreneur or business owner; in this chapter I'll delve deeper into what makes a good business owner, manager, leader; a good jockey, if you like. I use the analogy of a jockey because when you think of a thoroughbred racehorse, no matter how good it is, no matter its lineage or pedigree, it won't win races if it's ridden by a poor jockey. The same can be said of a business. It can have an excellent, competitively priced product or service, it can be well capitalized, it can be competitive, but if the person managing it isn't a good leader, its chances of success drop significantly.

I invest in businesses, and I invest in entrepreneurs, and that means carrying out enough due diligence to minimize the risks involved. It's incumbent on me to identify that there are enough positives in terms of the entrepreneur and the concept to warrant my attention. I don't invest just to make money—although I hate to lose it. I invest to help turn a business around, to make it more successful, to help it reach new heights. That's the challenge.

Anyone can invest in a business, then sit back and either watch it lose money or begin to provide dividends—that's called gambling. I always want the odds increasing in my favor. I look for companies where an entrepreneur and his or her management team are continually looking to improve. I want to see common sense, sound decisions, and leadership. What I don't want to see is a start-up committing to a twenty-year office lease at $60,000 a month because they want to emulate a company in Silicon Valley. Think that example sounds ridiculous? Well, senior management in a business I was recently involved in did just that—and that business no longer exists.

Remember, no matter how well a company is doing, it can always do better. And that's where sometimes backing good jockeys rather than good concepts can be a winning formula.

I am confident that almost anyone with a desire to become an entrepreneur can become a better leader or manager. One thing I found from the outset of my business career was that I learned more about what not to do in business from those who failed than from successful companies. The fact you are reading this book shows you are open to learning new ways to work on and in your business. That attitude will take you a long way in business, and you are not alone; we are all learning new things every day to ensure our businesses survive another day, another year. Welcome to the club.

Integrity and Respect, the Bedrock of Business

In my opinion the best businesspeople exhibit a deep-seated integrity. They respect their employees, their customers, their suppliers, and above all, themselves.

Let's assume you start your business today; how do you want to be remembered on the day you retire? When I first meet someone, I look for signs of respect. I search for an underlying sense of values and manners. As I mentioned was my habit when interviewing potential employees, whenever someone met with me at my office at Paychex's corporate offices and one of my assistants brought them a coffee or tea, I'd watch to see if they thanked the person. If they failed to show common decency by acknowledging the assistant, I would immediately question whether I wanted to do business with them or employ them. At the end of the meeting, if their cup was left on my desk for someone else to pick up or their chair was not put back neatly, I took it as another example of lack of respect.

Too often people are hung up on their own self-importance and dismiss as unimportant people who can't help them move their own selfish agenda forward. Respect is earned, not given.

I demanded the same level of respect from our trainees. Sometimes I used to sit by the cash register in the Paychex cafeteria at lunchtime and watch our employees coming in and out. I would call people out if they weren't clean shaven, their hair was messed up, or they weren't wearing a tie. I'd also watch for whether they cleaned up after themselves and pushed their chair back after leaving the table. I constantly demanded a certain level of basic respect and professionalism from our employees.

I haven't been CEO there for more than a decade, but if you visit Paychex's corporate offices today, or any Paychex office across the country, you will notice how clean and tidy it is and that all employees are well-presented. I am convinced you can build a level of professionalism into a corporation's culture to the point it will last forever, but you have to be committed and lead from the front. It won't just happen.

In case you are thinking I'm simply a guy with OCD, that I'm a neat freak, or that this is just one of my foibles, let me tell you why this has always been so important to me. Paychex clients expect the highest level of security, accuracy, and professionalism; they deserve no less when they entrust the company with their payrolls and their employees' privacy. You can't deliver that level of service consistently, or maybe at all, if professionalism at every level is not part of the organization's DNA.

Don't confuse having integrity with always having to be a nice guy or someone who's easy to walk over. You can be tough, very tough, but you can also be honest and fair. Remember, leading a business to success is not a popularity contest; it's about gaining respect for the way both you and your company act.

At the beginning of this section I asked, How do you want to be remembered on your last day working for your company? I can tell you, a lot will depend on how you begin your first day. Let's assume you start your business today. It's important on day one to consider what you want people to think, write, and say about you when you retire. If you're already in business, or even if you are a senior manager in a company, it's never too late to take a step back and reevaluate how you are managing yourself and your company.

Business Knowledge—What Should You Know?

As I said in chapter 1, I believe a good entrepreneur should have a background in the industry in which their business operates. Good managers and leaders, however, need a greater and deeper knowledge of the inner workings of their business—the cultural dynamics. They need the ability to inspire people at every level, while at the same time empowering other senior managers and departmental heads to spread their corporate vision throughout a company and ensure its implementation.

Most importantly, you need to know what you don't know. Huh? Let me explain. Often, entrepreneurs not only have large gaps in their business knowledge and experience but also are completely blind to their deficiencies. If you want to improve your chances of success, be honest with yourself and recognize the weaknesses in your business education and your business acumen, and seek help from a mentor or take courses to learn what you need to know. Let me tell you the story of my involvement with the owner of a tanning business (people, not leather).

When I invested in Zoom Tan, I was definitely backing the owner; Tony Toepfer had twenty-five years' experience in the tanning business. Originally from Chicago, Tony had started with a few salons and now the business was showing a profit and had good cash flow, but he was finding it tough to expand without an influx of capital.

Here was a case where an experienced businessperson with industry knowledge approached a competitive market with a new way of doing business that appealed to the target market. Some of Tony's pioneering efforts included opening smaller locations by making better use of space, introducing monthly subscription plans, advertising aggressively in an industry that traditionally did little advertising, and developing specialized software to assist managers in running tanning outlets.

My contribution, other than providing capital, has been to help Tony gain a better understanding of financial statements. As I discussed in chapter 3, I can't stress how important it is in any business to fully understand its finances. There is no way you can take an effective leadership or management role if you don't have a firm grip on the numbers.

You Have to Be Confident, Not Arrogant

It is important to wholeheartedly believe in your capabilities and demonstrate that belief. You need to have an unshakable personal conviction that what you are doing is correct; everything stems from that conviction.

Even before I seriously consider the validity of a business, an entrepreneur can turn me off completely and lose any chance of me becoming an investor in their business if they state they want to retain 51 percent of the company. What that tells me is that although they want to retain control, they want someone else to finance the risk. Let's explore that idea a little further.

When I ran Paychex, I never owned more than 50 percent of the company. After we merged, or consolidated, I only retained about 30 percent. Did that put me in a difficult or risky position? Not really; so many stockholders would have had to come together to vote me out, the chances of that happening were very slim. Unless, of course, I did something really dumb that hurt the company and threatened their investment. In which case I would have deserved to be ousted.

Demanding that you retain an unrealistic percentage of a company you are seeking investment for, or being unwilling to invest your own money in your company or mortgage your home to raise money, shows a lack of confidence in yourself and your company.

When it comes to ownership breakdown, it has to be logical. It has to make sense to the investor. I have people come to me and say they want to start a business and they are asking for $3 million; however, they are only willing to give up 10 percent of the company in return. What that tells me is that they are valuing the company at $30 million, which is usually ridiculous—especially if they have yet to open their doors. These ownership demands discredit investment seekers immediately in my eyes and prevent any serious discussion about their business concept.

Management

Let me tell you something. If you go to a company and the CEO is haggard, overscheduled, and busy, get the hell away from that company. Let me tell you another dirty little secret: the CEO should be the least busy of all the managers. But that does not mean he or she should be doing nothing. What it does mean is that a CEO should be working *on* the business, not *in* the business.

Look up the word *management* in a standard dictionary and it will be defined as the act of managing; a business dictionary will talk about it being the organization and coordination of the activities of a business. What all that means is that it's your job as a manager to look at the bigger picture while at the same time being the person who picks up a chocolate wrapper on the floor of your reception area that dozens of your employees failed to notice all day.

When I was CEO of Paychex, I would occasionally go down to our accounts payable office and ask for a bunch of invoices from our branches. I'd spend a little time going through them looking for anomalies. On one occasion I saw a monthly bill for cleaning temporary foyer rugs for our Philadelphia branch. The number of rugs we were being charged for seemed exceptionally high, so I asked soon-to-be-CEO Marty Mucci to call and see how many rugs they had at that branch. It turned out the company was triple billing us and the branch manager had been signing off on this every month without checking whether the billing was correct. The overcharging had cost the company several thousand dollars and could potentially have continued for years. If several branches were using the same company, the losses could have been multiplied.

The point of this story is that once I noticed this overbilling, a memo went out demanding that all branch managers check, or have an employee check, all invoices carefully. Good management is discovering your company's weaknesses and ensuring holes are plugged. It wasn't the first or the last time I discovered incorrect invoices. Profit is tough enough to make in the first place; the last thing you want is other people eroding your bottom line.

There are so many ways a company can lose, or waste, money. I remember once seeing that we were paying a million dollars a year for a computer program that tracked prospects and appointments, and allowed our salespeople to make presentations to potential clients. All our salespeople were given laptops, which they would utilize in making sales presentations; I was told this was important and that the sales department was very keen that they be used.

My first thought was, *I've got to see this in action*, so I asked for a salesperson to come and make a presentation to me as if I were a prospect. A woman from our sales team came into my office and sat across from me and spun her laptop around so I could see the screen and showed me a payroll, samples of what reports I, as a customer, would receive, what the checks looked like, etc. After a few seconds I said, "I can't see it very well from there. Could you come a little closer?" So she came around to my side of the desk and sat next to me, at which point I asked, "Do you always sit this close to someone you don't know?" And she said, "No, I don't usually use this. I use the paper one." My closing comment to the senior manager in the room was, "Case closed." It's easy to spend money once a company gets to a certain size and profitability; it's your job to ensure it's being spent wisely.

It is also your responsibility to be aware of what's going on in every aspect of your business. As I said earlier, to do this you need to have business knowledge, but you also have to be hands-on. Many entrepreneurs are so busy working *in* their business that they neglect to work *on* managing their business. Be hands-on—trust me, it works.

I remember several years ago working with a company called Safe Site. The company stored business documents, including client and medical records, for customers such as banks, insurance companies, and doctors' offices.

One day I got a call from my partner, and he told me we had a serious problem. I was floored when he informed me we owed over $2.3 million to the bank. In fact, our account was overdrawn. Incredibly, our chief financial officer had failed to mention this during any of our recent meetings. To cut a long story short, he was arrested by the FBI for kiting checks and electronic transactions between our branches. He had been writing checks for nonexistent funds and depositing them back and forth between accounts, relying on the three days it takes for the bank to process the checks. In this way he was able to access what amounted to an interest-free, unapproved loan. This is, of course, illegal, and it wasn't too long before the bank caught on to what he was doing.

His actions took us all by surprise, and I immediately realized it was unlikely that this was his only nefarious activity. I asked my partner to check with the IRS to see if we were behind on our payroll taxes, and sure enough, that call uncovered another $800,000 owed in taxes. Thankfully the company was able to recover from the debacle and was later sold for a sizeable profit.

The misconduct of the officer in the story above is another example of how easy it can be to take your eyes off what is happening in a company. Companies have a lot of moving parts, and a good owner/manager has to be able to recognize when something is amiss, when something doesn't add up, when their gut instinct begins to tell them something is not kosher.

Utilizing Advisors

People sometimes comment that managing a larger company or corporation is easier because you have a senior management team and a board of directors to turn to for advice and specialist skills or knowledge. They have a point, but companies of any size can pull together an advisory board at little to no cost. Look around at your business contacts, friends, fellow members of the local chamber of commerce maybe, for people with specific skills that could help you in your business. Your list could include a lawyer, an accountant, a tax expert, an industry specialist, an HR consultant, basically anyone whose expertise might help you run your business more efficiently and profitably. I suggest you ask them to meet quarterly and perhaps provide lunch or dinner, which could be as simple as pizza in your conference room.

An advisory board works better if you treat it as you would a board of directors. Prepare an agenda and brief departmental reports along with a balance sheet and income statement, and if possible, provide these to the board before you meet. This will allow them to arrive with questions and advice, based on your current situation. In this way you can run efficient meetings and require a minimum amount of time from your board.

Leadership

Effective leadership comes down to four steps an owner, CEO, or senior manager needs to nail:

1. Create the vision.
2. Sell the vision.
3. Execute the vision.
4. Monitor the results.

Do you consider yourself a good leader? Good leaders have a vision for their company and the ability to share that vision with everyone involved in their business. Ensure you are clear about your goals and objectives because it is up to you to take responsibility and lead by example.

I always practiced an open-door policy, and I wandered around the offices and sometimes ate at the cafeteria. I believe part of being a good leader is to be close to the business—very close. Don't ever get too far from the front of the business. I used to go to the training rooms every couple of weeks and test trainees to be sure they were learning what they needed to know to be successful for themselves and for the company.

Good leaders must be able to create a vision and sell that vision strongly enough to get honest and enthusiastic buy-in from senior managers, who can then sell the vision down the line. At that point, if everyone gets behind the vision, the goals, and the objectives, then the vision needs to be executed. To do that, you as the leader and the other leaders at all levels of your company need strong communication skills. Remember, one of the biggest complaints put forward by employees is lack of communication.

Good leaders are not necessarily born; they can be made, but they do have to be able to show empathy, be decisive, know how to hire and trust the right people, recognize and develop existing talent, delegate rather than do everything themselves, collaborate with the senior management team and others, and never be afraid to ask for help.

Persistence Pays

One of the keys to success is being persistent, not giving up at the first sign of problems or challenges. I remember a business I invested in that required patience and persistence, not to mention additional capital investment to survive.

I invested in a company called Ultra-Scan that was founded in 1987; it had developed an ultrasound scanner, similar to those used in medical applications, to identify fingerprints. I had invested $20 million, but sales never lived up to expectations due to the high cost to the end user.

This could have easily been a time to cut my losses, but the CEO called me one day and said he'd had an idea. He explained that our current technology was designed to only scan two fingers but that the FBI was interested in us developing four-finger identification. He needed another $5 million and a year or two to develop what the FBI wanted.

Sometimes you have to stick with the plan, so I put in the capital and increased my equity position. Time passed, and I got another call from him, this time to tell me that a company called Qualcomm wanted to buy the company for $65 million. My patience, persistence, and belief in the concept was rewarded with a significant profit. Like the song says, you've got to know when to hold them and when to fold them.

Get Noticed for Good Management

People who know me well know that I rarely if ever boast about my successes in business; however, there are a few honors Paychex was given of which I am extremely proud. In 2004, as I was in the process of stepping down as CEO, Paychex was recognized for the third time running as one of the 100 Best Companies to Work For by *Fortune* magazine, which also named us as one of the most admired companies in the country. In the same year we were listed as one of the top training companies in the United States, an honor Paychex continues to hold to this day. Finally, on more than one occasion *Forbes* magazine honored Paychex by listing it as one of the best-managed companies in America. I was also listed as one of the top three executives in America for three years running in the early 2000s by *Forbes* magazine based on my total compensation package versus the company's stock price growth.

It's this last point I wish to explore. I take issue with the massive salaries many CEOs make, which are often not linked to the company's performance. I always took a very conservative salary and never felt the need to continually take stock options. It is rare after a company goes public that Wall Street allows the founder to remain as CEO for any length of time. However, for over twenty years after Paychex went public, I continued to lead the company and offered shareholders exceptional value and return on investment through my modest compensation package when compared with other CEOs of major corporations.

Leadership takes many forms, but in essence you have to take a step back and put the needs of your company, your customers, your shareholders and investors, and your employees first. I achieved my vision for Paychex by being the best leader and manager I could be, and I'm gratified that the management strategies I introduced at Paychex over the years are still effective today.

We adopted the same management practices when I purchased the Buffalo Sabres, and in 2007, when the team won the Presidents' Trophy, *ESPN The Magazine* voted us the best-managed professional franchise across all sports.

Takeaways

- Anyone with a desire to become an entrepreneur can become a better leader and manager.
- Success depends on you. You need to know your stuff. Good managers know their businesses intimately.
- Be realistic when assessing the market share your business might achieve.
- Investors bet on good jockeys, not just good business concepts.
- The best businesspeople have deep-seated integrity. Respect is earned, not given.
- Ask yourself how you want to be remembered after you retire from your business.

- You need to believe in your own capabilities and demonstrate that belief.
- It's possible to build an organizational culture that can last forever.
- Good managers work on their businesses, not just in them.
- Good leaders can create a vision, sell that vision, execute it, and continually monitor the company's progress toward the vision.
- You are responsible not only for your own actions but also for those of your company.
- Two keys to success are patience and persistence.
- Create an advisory board to provide access to additional experience and skills.

EIGHT

A GOOD DEAL FOR EVERYONE

I suppose my idea of a good deal for everyone started a short time after I launched Paychex, or Paymaster, as it was originally named. Originally, I had no intention of providing payroll processing services outside of my hometown Rochester, but an ex-colleague, Phil Wehrheim, from EAS approached me and asked to partner with me; we struck a fifty-fifty partnership deal (without lawyers), and he opened offices servicing Buffalo, Syracuse, and Albany. Then Chuck Wollmer, the employee of a client, came to me wanting to get in on the action. I was happy to offer him a partnership, but he wanted a franchise. I'll go into more detail about how we negotiated Paychex's very first franchise deal later in this chapter, but that was how we started to grow into more than a small local business. Word got around and other people I knew well and trusted, like Bob Sebo, approached me asking to become a partner or buy a franchise.

Making it a good deal for everyone was at the heart of Paychex from the beginning. It was ingrained into the company's corporate philosophy, it made sense, and it was important to me. Growing a national organization simply happened one territory at a time; by the time we consolidated into one company, there were seventeen of us, both partners and franchisees, and as I mentioned earlier, it felt more like a fraternity than a business. That climate could not have been achieved if each person hadn't felt they were getting a good deal. Those who stuck with the company after it went public, or later left but held on to their stock, are now extremely wealthy, so without question they got the ultimate good deal.

I've always believed that if you can manage to negotiate a deal both sides feel good about, or at least think is reasonable under the circumstances, then it's a win-win, and win-wins can lead to long-term relationships. I've never agreed with business gurus who treat business like war. Win at all costs seems to be their mantra, but "wins" like that are often short-lived. Any relationship built on someone having to be the loser can never be good for a business in the long run.

I've built my success on always trying to create a good deal for all concerned. That's not to say I don't want to get a good deal for myself—a higher discount, better terms—but if it's not a satisfactory deal for the vendor, their ability to deliver may be affected, perhaps quality will suffer, or in a worst-case scenario, they will go out of business. If that seems extreme, think about the many reported cases of suppliers going out of business after being pressured into delivering large quantities of a product at unrealistic discounts by mega retailers.

My approach to negotiation is to figure out what the other person needs in terms of a number, or other options, and do my best to provide them with an offer that isn't too far from what they are expecting. How do I do this? I'm a good listener and I do my homework. The more educated I am about their situation, the better position it puts me in to make a deal that benefits both them and me. Common ground is where the best deals are made, ones that stand the test of time. People walk away from one-sided deals and nobody wins. Good deals can be arrived at where the parties are equally happy, or even equally unhappy.

In business there can be many winners in any industry, and that's a good thing; read my views on competition in chapter 5. This is contrary to politics, where you run against another candidate and you either win or lose. During my stint as a politician, when I ran for governor of New York three times, I met many unprincipled and corrupt politicians for whom winning was the only goal, rather than serving the constituency they were supposed to be representing and by whom they were elected. Some of them lost elections, others lost grace, and a few ended up in prison. I am glad to report that after fifty-plus years in business, it's my experience that any time you can get a good deal for everyone, it will turn out to be good for your business and increase your chances of long-term success.

"Win at all costs" people are tempted to do things that are over the top, illegal, immoral, or unethical. You don't have to do that in business. But that's not to say businesspeople don't act that way. You always need to be on your guard for the unscrupulous.

Divorce: The Ultimate Negotiation

Negotiation is far easier when everyone is on the same side, even though they will still be negotiating for the best deal they can achieve. My "good deal for everyone" philosophy extends to my personal life. Horror stories of wealthy people suffering financially during a divorce are legendary. It's often said that the only winners in a divorce are the lawyers. Well, I've been divorced three times. Twice I paid both sides of the legal fees, and for my third divorce I paid my side of the legal fees. My last divorce was in 2007, so what I'm about to tell you is not ancient history in terms of cost. The total I paid in legal fees for all three divorces combined was less than $6,000. Why? Because I sat down with each of my wives and worked out a reasonable settlement before the lawyers became involved and started playing us against each other and turning everything into a crusade.

I firmly believe that in almost all cases it is possible to find common ground and work out a deal where both parties get most or all of what they want. The worst-case scenario, if you approach everything fairly, is a deal that both parties are equally unhappy with, but they can accept.

I remember when my first wife, Gloria, and I sat down to discuss our separation and divorce at the kitchen table. I told her I had a liquidity issue, that coming up with a cash settlement would be difficult. She in turn said that what she wanted was for me to give her the New York City Paychex franchise, which at the time was one of the few I hadn't sold. In addition, she wanted me to train her to run it and provide her financial assistance until it broke even. My first consideration was whether I thought she could handle the franchise, but I knew she had great social skills and would be excellent at bringing in business. Although I knew the computer room would scare the life out of her, I knew we could help her with that aspect of the business.

After some consideration I came to the conclusion that this deal could be good for both of us. As it turned out, she was a great franchisee and made a success of the business, so much so that after the consolidation she ended up owning 5 percent of Paychex. If she still held those stocks today, they would be worth more than $1 billion—now I'd say that was a good deal, wouldn't you?

The Day I Broke the "Never Negotiate from an Ultimatum" Rule

There is a saying, "Never negotiate from an ultimatum," and in principle I agree with it. If you are trying to buy a car and you tell the salesperson that you are only willing to pay a certain amount or you will walk, then you had better be prepared to walk. In reality, however, you may be closer to a deal than you think. If you are both willing to give a little, a good deal could be achieved by both parties.

But let me tell you the story of when I broke the rule and it worked. It was when I took Paychex from being a bunch of partners and franchisees and turned it into a corporation. We all met in Nassau to discuss consolidating into a single company. It posed a significant challenge: in addition to me, there were sixteen partners and franchisees who had a stake in Paychex. If I wanted them all to agree on consolidation, each and every one had to believe they were getting a fair deal. The big question was, how would I decide who got what percentage of the new company?

There was simply no way I could have negotiated a deal with sixteen partners and franchisees with big egos who possessed a skewed view of their actual worth. It would have been a moving target; as soon as I made a deal with one person, I knew details would get back to someone whom I'd already reached a deal with and then that person would want to renegotiate.

My only chance was to create an acceptable no-negotiation situation. Prior to the meeting I sat down with Bob Beegen, my partner in Detroit, and Philip Wehrheim, my partner in upstate New York, and we made a list of everyone's territories. Against each, we noted what they had accomplished to date and assessed their future potential. Based on this initial information, we noted what we felt each person should receive by way of shares compared to the others. This first step was crucial because it gave us a base from which to adjust for factors outside the primary formula.

The most important thing I decided was that I would not negotiate with anyone. With the help of Bob and Phil, I thrashed out a good deal for all parties the best we could by taking into consideration the size of each territory, how well the territory had been managed, and its profitability. The formula we used was complex and interconnected; changing one individual's share of the new company would require us to reassess everyone else's. The ripple effect was unthinkable. I also knew the minute we started negotiating with one of the sixteen, we would end up having to negotiate with them all—and that wasn't going to happen.

I handed out the offers, and the next day we gathered around a boardroom table in a private room at the hotel. I opened with, "This is it, this is the deal—we're not changing it. If you don't want to join us, that's okay. We'll protect your city and we won't go into your territory. No hard feelings."

I went to each person in turn and asked them whether they wanted in or out. By the time I finished, every single person had agreed to accept the package and join the new Paychex corporation.

To reemphasize what a good deal it was, if every owner still owned the share of the company they were given that day, the one who received the lowest number of shares would now own shares in Paychex worth $250 million.

No-Nonsense Negotiating

I always attempted to create win-win situations when doing any deal, but especially in major negotiations. Such was the case in 2002, when Paychex acquired Advantage Payroll Services Inc., based in Chicago, for $240 million in cash. This was a significant acquisition.

What was more interesting than the acquisition itself was the way it happened. I was at an investment conference in Chicago and knew the company was owned by a venture capital company that wanted to take them public. While in Chicago, I called the general partner of the firm and asked if I could meet with him. As soon as we started to discuss a potential purchase, I realized his company didn't want the hassle or cost of going public. Venture capital firms often want to realize a quick return on their investment.

From my perspective, I had to figure out whether I could afford to make the purchase and whether that amount was worth spending to take out a competitor with forty branches that was growing faster than we were. The answer, of course, was yes. I calculated the approximate cost involved in taking the company public, took into consideration the current value of the company and also its potential value after going public, and came up with what I thought was a genuinely good offer. Within forty-five minutes I'd made him an offer and he accepted.

The key to good negotiating is to do your homework and know, before you start talking, what the other person is likely to consider a good price. You also have to know what price you feel represents a good deal for your company.

There have been complete books written about the art of negotiating, but when you strip away the smoke and mirrors, it's simply about finding that sweet spot where both parties feel they can sleep content. Anything else is fool's gold.

Now, you may be thinking that it can't be as simple as that, and you'd be correct. The basic agreement can be reached quickly with the method I've described above, but then accountants and lawyers have to carry out their due diligence and pull together the paperwork. Just don't bring the lawyers in too soon. Negotiating only becomes complicated if you let it or if you let people being paid by the hour become involved.

Working with Vendors

In business, there are a lot of people whose services you may have to retain from time to time. There are lawyers, accountants, advertising agencies, PR agencies, manufacturers, suppliers, contractors . . . The list goes on. Let's call them vendors. While I admit most businesses need to use these vendors, they can become one of the biggest drains on your operating budget, especially those who charge by the hour. I particularly dislike those.

As an example, let's look at lawyers. Lawyers in particular are exceptionally costly, and their fees have a habit of escalating in a most alarming fashion unless you are watching them carefully. I once had a legal firm work for me over maybe two or three months, but they failed to send us a bill until fifteen months later. The amount escalated to an insane amount, and I had no way of monitoring their hours or productivity.

You have no idea whether they are overcharging you or doing unnecessary work. One thing you need to watch out for is their habit of charging you $200–$250 an hour for a junior associate earning $30 an hour. And don't get me started on the use of boilerplate or templated documents that are charged out as though they were created from scratch.

When you use any professional firm, make sure you really need them, because sometimes they can actually get in the way. While negotiating my very first franchise agreement in the early days of Paychex, my new franchisee and I sat in my conference room with our respective lawyers. After a few hours I came to the realization that the only people arguing were the lawyers. I asked them to leave, and my new franchisee and I struck a deal in ten minutes. We shook hands, walked out, and told the lawyers to simply handle the paperwork. It wasn't the first or the last time I metaphorically, or even literally, threw a lawyer out of my office.

Working with advertising agencies, PR firms, and just about any other company that bills by the hour is hazardous to your bottom line. Parameters need to be set. When dealing with any such vendor, my advice is to insist on monthly detailed billing. You have to build a relationship that works in both your favor and theirs.

Negotiation and the Pregnant Pause

As I stated earlier, one of my favorite negotiation tools is the pregnant pause. I've used it when interviewing staff, buying cars, even when trying to decide on which movie to watch. In fact, I employ this simple technique regularly across a wide range of situations. In essence, it's a well-placed pause, or period of silence, which encourages someone to agree with what you have just said or suggested. It's effective in closing sales deals, but also in getting people to tell you more than they might otherwise be willing to share. Police officers and detectives are adept at using the pregnant pause.

I've used it countless times, but on one occasion it was particularly effective. About a year after I purchased the Buffalo Sabres hockey franchise, a major mistake was made by a senior manager that cost me a great deal of money.

Toward the end of our first season I learned about contract addendums. Prior to the then-current collective bargaining agreement in the NHL, there were standard player contracts, but almost every player had an addendum that modified the standard part of the contract. This meant that when you traded for a player, you had to study the addendum to discover what you were buying into.

For example, a player might have had written into their agreement that they would receive a bonus if they scored twenty goals during the season. If upon being traded midseason the player had scored nineteen goals, the two teams would stipulate during the trade conference that the old team would pay 19/20ths of the bonus. Today riders are not allowed on contracts, but back then it could be a major issue.

Unbeknownst to me, in my first year with the Sabres, we had traded for a player who had a rider, or addendum, on his contract. He was a young player and not playing well. Our negotiating team had not read the contract thoroughly, or at least not the rider, which stated he was entitled to an additional $250,000 if he played in a specified number of games. When we bought him, he had just two games left before qualifying for this bonus. It wasn't until after the season ended that it came to our CEO, Larry Quinn's, attention that we owed this player a quarter million dollars.

At the end of the season I invited Larry Quinn, Dan DiPofi, our chief operating officer, and Darcy Regier, the general manager, down to my Florida home for a meeting to review and discuss our performance. Initially it was just the senior management team, as Darcy wasn't due to arrive until the following day. We had a very productive day. After a long discussion and analysis, we developed and agreed on a plan to drastically reduce season ticket prices and to introduce the concept of variable pricing for individual game tickets. Satisfied with our efforts, I suggested we go watch the playoffs at a local restaurant.

That evening at dinner Dan informed me about the situation with the bonus. Larry had told him to hold off until breakfast the following day, but it had been eating away at Dan all day, so when he got me alone at the bar, he spilled the beans. I stormed up to Larry and said, "When were you going to tell me about this?" Larry replied that he was hoping we could have a nice dinner and deal with it the next day. I asked him what the heck we were going to do about it, and he pleaded, "Before you get upset, let's talk about it tomorrow morning after we've spent some time talking with Darcy about the team."

The next morning, we gathered in my small sunroom, and after the normal greetings and pleasantries, I immediately opened with, "So, do we owe a games-played bonus for this player?" I sat there, and they all looked at each other and no one answered until Darcy said, "Yes." I asked how much of it San Jose would cover, since he came from that team. Darcy answered, "None of it." I then asked him who had reviewed the rider and got no answer. In fact, no one said a word. Four adults sat around a small table in a resplendently bright and cheery sun-drenched room in excruciatingly uncomfortable silence—at least for three of them.

I let the silence hang, and hang. I watched Larry, Dan, and Darcy squirm, as if they were all about to melt into pools of steaming liquid on the tile floor; especially Darcy, whose department had ultimate responsibility for contracts. Still I said nothing—for a full forty-five minutes—and neither did anyone else.

Eventually Larry could stand it no more. He got up to walk out onto the patio and crashed right into the glass doors, smashing his head, bouncing off, and falling to the floor. Jumping to his feet but now sporting a large bump on his head, he reached for his water and still the silence continued. Sometime later Darcy finally spoke up and said, "Tom, do you want me to reimburse you for the loss?" I thought for a moment or two and then responded, "That won't be necessary. Let's move on." And we went on with our business as normal.

The long silence, or pregnant pause, is something I have used extensively in business and is one of the most effective tools in an entrepreneur's arsenal when used correctly. In this case I used it to remind my team to respect my money, respect my investment, and not be cavalier or careless with our resources. I expect the same from any company in which I invest and any charity to which I donate money and time.

People often ask me how to deal with someone who is employing the pregnant pause, so I'll share it with you: you have to have the strength of character to outlast them. It's not easy to sit in silence; it's in our nature to fill the void. But if you don't and someone else does, you can learn a lot of useful information. But never try to outlast me—seriously.

Try practicing the pregnant pause in personal circumstances, perhaps when you have stated your preference of restaurant to go to for dinner or what movie you'd like to watch. Let the silence hang, and more often than not, you will get the outcome you desire.

Another time it can be employed is after asking a question to which you already know the answer or when you know the answer you wish to hear. I used to get accused of this constantly at Paychex. It is a great way of seeing whether people are being honest and consistent. It also offers you an opportunity to get differing opinions. On occasion I have been known to change my mind after asking such a question, but again, only on occasion.

Asking Direct Questions

Another negotiation or interview technique I frequently use is to ask very direct questions. People think I do this to make them feel uncomfortable, but they are legitimate questions; I just ask them in a very direct way.

Two interview questions I often used are, "How much money do you make at your current position?" and "If we ask you to relocate, will your spouse support the move?"

When I'm looking to acquire or invest in a business, I ask things like, "What's the biggest concern you have about your business?" or "How much of your own money have you put into the business?" Further along in negotiations I might ask, "If we go ahead and proceed to acquire your company, we would like you to continue working for three to five years. Are you willing to do that?"

One question I've asked on several occasions when mentoring the owner of a company I am investing in is, "Do you really think your son-in-law [or niece or whoever] is the best person to be marketing director of the company?"

Questions like these are meant to put someone on the spot so they are forced to make a decision or perhaps provide information they might otherwise prefer not to disclose. They also force the person to deal with reality and come to terms with situations they might otherwise avoid facing.

Previously we talked about the pregnant pause and its effectiveness. A word of warning: do not employ it if you are asked a direct question. Direct questions require immediate answers; hesitating can imply a reluctance to answer the question. This will lead to suspicion as to the accuracy and honesty of your eventual reply.

Winning Graciously

I've always tried to win graciously and disagree with those who feel the need to rub salt into the wounds of people they have beaten in the game of business. There is zero upside to that behavior. You win some and you lose some; you make good decisions and you unfortunately from time to time make poor decisions. The art of being successful in business is to make more of the former and fewer of the latter.

Here is an example of someone who did not lose graciously. In 1981, ADP (Automatic Data Processing) showed interest in buying Paychex. They seemed serious, so I went to Roseland, New Jersey, to meet with two senior VPs and an acquisitions manager. They offered $20 million, but there was a caveat: the purchase contract was based on an earnout over a three-year period. This meant Paychex would have to meet certain goals before receiving the total amount; in other words, responsibility without authority. When I told the acquisitions manager that there was no way I was going to take that deal, he slammed his fist on the table and said, "You're going to be forever sorry." I calmly replied, "We'll see what happens." That's another way to close down negotiations quickly.

I had no appetite to go back and reopen any discussions with ADP, especially with that individual. Paychex grew to be worth more than one thousand times what they were offering back then, so I didn't and don't feel at all sorry. But to this day I still treat ADP with the respect they deserve—that's winning graciously.

Fun and Responsibility

My philosophy of making things a good deal for everyone goes back to my early days as an entrepreneur and includes everyone from business partners and employees to customers and vendors. Outside of business deals this also involves having fun with people, while at the same time holding people responsible for their actions.

Business should have a fun side, and I am known for the pranks and practical jokes I play on the people I care about, and the pranks people have played on me from time to time. In chapter 6, I shared several humorous stories relating to the training we carried out at

Paychex, but now let me tell you about a few times when fun and business came together in perfect harmony.

Once a month we had an officers' meeting. I remember on one occasion there were about twelve senior managers in the room, and we were talking about how many clients we were gaining compared to our attrition rate. One zone manager announced seriously, "We've got to sell more than we lose," as if this were a pearl of profound wisdom. I said, "Well, that's a revelation."

Forever after, we'd start each meeting with managers reading their "revelations," and I was never short of ones to choose from, including a wonderful example from our chief financial officer who stated, after I asked him to tell me our current cash position, "Somewhere between four hundred and eight hundred million dollars." That statement came back to haunt him for many years, as did these sage statements from other senior managers: "You've got to hire good people" and one of my favorites, "To have more clients, we have to sell more clients." It may have been fun, but it also made people think before uttering what they considered to be a thoughtful insight.

Although I like to have fun for fun's sake, I have also throughout my business life used it as a means to issue a life lesson to those I felt were in need of a kick up the proverbial backside.

Senior management occupied the fourth floor at Paychex's corporate office, and we had a tradition of celebrating birthdays with cake and ice cream on the Friday closest to someone's birthday. Gene Polisseni, who was head of HR, started this tradition, and I supported it as a good morale booster. They were fairly innocuous events, unless it was your first birthday with the company, in which case you were expected to wear a party hat complete with a rubber band to hold it in place. I didn't start this particular mild form of hazing, but I did enforce it because, well, it was hilarious.

Shortly before Marty Mucci took over as CEO, he celebrated his birthday and the time came for him to don the hat. He refused and was duly jeered by all present. He eventually picked up the hat, touched it to his head, and threw it back down on the table and said, "Okay, I wore the hat!" I didn't say a word—not then, anyway.

At the next officers' meeting I brought up for discussion the color of our checks, which had always been Paychex blue, our corporate color. A conversation ensued, and I could see Marty was unhappy with the topic and wanted to say something. Now, one of my golden and intractable rules in meetings is that only one person is allowed to talk at a time, but when Marty launched into why he thought changing the color of the checks was ridiculous, everyone else in the room started talking to each other and ignored him completely.

Much to Marty's astonishment, I let it continue for a short while and then said, "Okay, let's move on." At which point Marty started to remake his point: "I think it's foolish . . ." and everyone started talking again. When this happened for a third time, Marty, who was beside himself, said, "Can anybody hear me in this room?" The room went completely silent. I quietly turned to Marty and said, "Next time you'll wear the f—ing hat."

That's not the end of the story. When I retired Marty sent me a card, and inside the envelope was a crumpled party hat. I never acknowledged receiving it, but sometime later when I was visiting Paychex I went into his office and left the hat on his chair. Nothing was ever said.

There was never mean intent in the pranks, even when I nearly destroyed my best friend's car. Gene Polisseni drove a Mercedes-Benz SL sports car all winter long in Rochester, New York, and that was quite unusual at the time. One day when I drove into work I saw a large crane that was starting construction on the addition of our new corporate offices. It gave me an idea, and I asked the contractor to build a platform large enough to hold a car. Then one day we sent Gene out to lunch for a business meeting and got his spare set of car keys from his wife.

When he returned to the office, his bright-red Mercedes was five stories above our building. It was windy, and the car was swinging back and forth, and I thought, *Jeez, this might become a $75,000 joke if it hits the pavement.* Gene, however, was unflappable; all he said was, "Boy, I wish I'd thought of that." People talked about it for years, especially regulars at the restaurant across the street who couldn't believe their eyes.

Business doesn't have to be deadly serious all the time; you are allowed to have some fun. My no-nonsense approach more often than not looks for humor that contains a message or a test, be it of character, personality, or intelligence.

Takeaways

- A good deal for everyone can and should be achievable.
- The more you understand about the other party's situation, the more likely you will reach a good deal.
- Occasionally a good deal can leave all parties equally unhappy.
- Negotiation is easier when everyone is on the same side.
- In the world of business there can be many winners, unlike in politics.
- Sometimes a good deal for everyone has to be nonnegotiable.
- Be cautious when working with a vendor who charges by the hour. Monitor all hourly work and set parameters.

- Build relationships with vendors that work in your favor, and theirs.
- Lawyers' fees escalate quickly; watch them carefully.
- Be aware that lawyers sometimes charge hourly rates for creating contracts that are in fact boilerplate templates. Review contracts to ascertain how much is specific to your situation.
- Negotiate with lawyers and accountants who charge out junior associates at hundreds of dollars an hour for doing basic administrative tasks.
- Always read the small print in lawyers' contracts. It's their world, and you may be at a disadvantage.
- Leave lawyers out of the negotiation phase and only bring them in to deal with due diligence and contracting.
- Never let lawyers get in the way of a good deal. Remember, you are the client.
- Learn the art of the pregnant pause and use it shrewdly.
- Never be a sore loser, and win graciously.
- Humor and fun come in many forms; they can be used to send messages, correct errant behavior, and test people's character, personality, and intelligence.

NINE

BUILDING A POSITIVE PUBLIC IMAGE

When you think of any company, even one you don't necessarily know well, you will instantly have an opinion, or perhaps a feeling about the brand, be it good or bad. Think of Starbucks, or the Nike swoosh; think of Microsoft and Apple; think of Walmart. As you read those names you will instantly have a gut feeling about each company. They have a profile, an image, that in your mind is either negative or positive. Unlike the companies mentioned above, your company may be new, but it's important to build its image from day one. And if your existing company is suffering from a blah image, the following tips and advice may help you kick its profile up a notch or two.

Never underestimate the power of your public profile to influence everything in your company: employee morale, motivation, retention, recruitment, customer satisfaction, sales, media attention, investor interest, and more. Your public image is based on everything you say and do and on your overall corporate culture and philosophy.

BUILT, NOT BORN

Let me outline some basic strategies that will help your business enjoy the type of respect and loyal following Paychex has enjoyed for forty-eight years from employees, customers, and shareholders.

Picking a Name

The name of your company can say a lot about you, so be careful if you are choosing a name for your new company or you plan to undertake a rebranding process. Paychex's original name was Paymaster, a name we had to change when we became a national company because there was another company with the same name that was already established. This turned out to be a blessing in disguise; almost fifty years later, is there anyone who knows the meaning of the term *paymaster*? In case you are wondering, a paymaster was the military official who handled paying salaries or wages to military personnel.

Looking back, before I started bringing on partners and franchisees, I was focused entirely on providing payroll services to the Rochester area; given that, it would have been easy to have decided to call my company Rochester Payroll Services, which of course would not have worked nationally.

I've seen other entrepreneurs use their name and attach "and Associates," which I would suggest you avoid. It does not sound as professional as you might think and can appear a little fake. It will not help build your corporate profile, and I for one would never invest in a company using that naming formula.

People often ask me how we came up with the name Paychex. It was simple. I gathered six or seven of my colleagues together, and

144

we wrote names on a blackboard and someone wrote the words *Pay* and *Checks* on the board and that evolved into Paychex. What made it a good name was that it fell right in line with the other services we offered, such as 401(k)s and employee handbooks; everything we did centered around the paycheck.

When you are considering what to call yourself, be cognizant of where you think you would like your business to go in the future. Names should have longevity and shouldn't restrict what services and products you might sell in the future and at what location or locations. I think the name Paychex gives a higher profile and more positive public image than Paychex's payroll processing competitor ADP, which stands for Automatic Data Processing. A good name is very important to your public profile. Choose wisely.

A Positive Profile Starts at Home

Employees come and go. Every time a valued employee leaves your company there is a cost in lost production, retraining for the new employee, and an orientation period where the new employee absorbs your corporate culture. Underlying this is the concern that when an employee leaves your employment, they take with them an impression of your company, which they may share with others, and you want to be sure it will be favorable. The best advice I can give you is to treat your employees fairly and never let difficult situations linger; the longer they linger, the more they escalate.

Some business owners fail to recognize the return on investment they can get by having happy employees who believe in, and have pride in, their company.

Act Professionally

Acting professionally sounds like obvious advice, but many businesses miss this basic principle. They are so busy with all the other aspects of their business they fail to notice the things that customers see when they walk through their doors or call their company. Your premises need to be tidy, clean, and orderly at all times, even if your clients never visit your offices. If you always appear and act professional, you will *be* professional, and that will come across in the very essence of your business.

Your employees should present themselves in a positive and professional manner. Their physical appearance and the way they interact with clients is important. Employees at Paychex knew I would notice if they hadn't shaved or if their desk was messy. It was written in stone that clients were to be treated with respect; any employee interacting with customers knew how they should treat them. These expectations were built into the corporate culture, and therefore the corporate image and profile. Even employees who did not interact with customers were expected to dress and act professionally, and that's what makes a public image work, when you are not doing it just for the public.

We've covered the internal culture that creates your public profile, but what about people who call in by telephone? We talked about first impressions, and sometimes the first impression someone gets about your company is when they call your number. Employees answering the phone should use a set script so there is continuity when customers and inquirers call your company. It should never come across as if it is being read; train people to learn the script and make it natural. Always choose front-desk people with friendly, outgoing personalities who are also highly professional. When customers or prospective customers call your company, you want them to experience your corporate image.

Smaller companies and extremely large companies often use automated answering systems or services. If you go this route, ensure it is user friendly and preferably offers callers the opportunity of talking to a live person.

As a closing thought on acting professionally, instigate a policy of always underpromising and overdelivering; it will stand you in good stead with whomever your company interacts.

Vendor Relationships

If the average person can spread bad news and reviews about your company from one end of the world to the other in a nanosecond via social media, a vendor who has long-overdue, unpaid invoices can spread the word to your other suppliers. That can damage many important relationships on which you may rely heavily. Always ensure you pay vendors on time and build a reputation of being fair and prompt in all your dealings.

A Professional Image

I talked earlier about brand image and how people make immediate assumptions based on what they see and even what they feel about a company. The same is true when you hand someone your business card, or they receive a letter from you. If your card is poorly designed and printed on thin card stock and your logo is amateurish, what does that say about you and your company?

Your website can be the first thing people see when searching for your company, so again, it needs to be professionally designed and kept up to date. If your company uses brochures, flyers, and other promotional material or produces reports, they all need to not only look professional but also be written in proficient English. My advice is to use professional designers and writers—they earn their money.

Get on Board with Social Media

Social media is important to every business; an unsatisfied customer can post a detrimental review on any number of sites, and in a blink of an eye it can be read by thousands. Monitoring social media sites frequented by your customer base should be a responsibility of someone in your company, potentially a full-time job, depending on your size.

Your website needs to be professional, easy to navigate, useful to clients, and constantly kept up to date. I know I'm in danger of citing the obvious, but no one looks up your number in a phone book anymore.

Inexpensive Profile Boosting

Advertising your product or company in newspapers can be expensive, but you can cost-effectively build your profile locally by announcing corporate milestones and senior management appointments and promotions. This strategy can regularly keep your company front and center in the eyes of your community.

The Best Form of Advertising

The best advertising comes from satisfied customers. I mentioned in a previous chapter how we marketed Paychex's services by approaching accountants and encouraging them to recommend us to their clients. Third-party referencing will raise your company's profile and also establish a high degree of credibility. Approach satisfied customers and ask for testimonials and leads to other sales prospects.

Media Relationships

How do you deal with media during difficult times? My immediate response is never argue with anyone who buys ink by the barrel. In all seriousness, it's always best to avoid disputes whenever possible. If something happens in your business that detrimentally affects your customers or results in some other scandal, you need to immediately own your shortcomings. The key is to quickly come up with a plan of action that will rectify the issues those affected suffered.

Think about the way car manufacturers announce recalls. They try to get out ahead of the problem by providing a plan to literally fix the problem no matter the cost. There may be some short-term pain for car owners, but once the issue is fixed at no cost to them, they are usually placated.

Denying a serious issue, if one occurs, can end up being worse for your public profile and image. It's not the problem that is the main concern; it's how you respond to it. Transparency can help mitigate the hit your corporate image might take.

Networking Builds Profile

The best people to promote your corporate image are you and your senior management staff. Networking at local events hosted by business associations or other organizations, including nonprofits, offers an opportunity to promote your company and build its image in the community.

I will warn you, however, to be careful of any time commitments you make to not-for-profit organizations; they have a habit of absorbing as much of your time as you allow them to, and then some. One strategy some business owners employ is to involve their spouses in charitable work on behalf of the company.

Politics and Business—Can They Mix?

I would advise you not to become involved with local, state, or federal politics through your business. This is a sweeping statement, and a lot depends on your specific business and your industry. In some cases, some level of involvement may be unavoidable, but in general be careful about your support of and any financial contributions to politicians, and don't be pulled into their fights and controversies. A safer approach, in cases where you have little choice, may be to give to multiple political organizations or candidates, to show support to the democratic process and thus achieve corporate exposure.

Be Charitable When You Can

If your company grows to a point or is already at a point where it can make charitable donations, I suggest you not be totally altruistic with your charitable giving. No matter your motivation for philanthropy, for the sake of your investors, your shareholders, and your own future, I recommend you take advantage of any PR opportunities that are offered or that you can think of.

A word of warning: be careful not to overcommit. Start slowly and build your support as your company can afford the financial outlay.

—

The title of my autobiography will be *A Good Deal for Everyone*, which is also the title of chapter 8 in this book. The phrase encapsulates my entire corporate philosophy, which in turn formed the basis of Paychex's public profile. Make no mistake: nothing helps you build a positive corporate image better than always being seen to focus on ensuring all your customers, vendors, and employees get a good deal that works for them and, of course, you.

Building a positive public image is important to your company. If you don't build one, you may discover all too late that a public image has been thrust upon you that is a lot less flattering than one you might have been able to create.

Takeaways

- Never underestimate the power of your public profile to influence everything in your company.
- Your public image is based on everything you say and do and on your overall corporate culture and philosophy.
- A good name is very important to your public profile. Choose wisely.
- A positive profile starts at home.
- Underpromise and overdeliver; it will stand you in good stead with whomever your company interacts.

- Focus on ensuring all your customers, vendors, and employees get a good deal that works for them and for you.
- Always ensure you pay vendors on time and build a reputation of being fair and prompt in all your dealings.
- People make immediate assumptions based on what they see and even what they feel about your company.
- Get on board with social media and treat it seriously.
- The best advertising comes from satisfied customers.
- When it comes to serious problems in your business, it's not the problem that is the main concern; it's how you fix it.
- Don't underestimate the benefits of networking in your community.
- Don't become involved with local, state, or federal politics through your business unless you have to, and then be bipartisan if possible.
- With charitable giving, start slowly and build your support as your company can afford the financial outlay.
- If you don't build your own public image, one may be thrust upon you.

TEN

ONLY DIAMONDS ARE FOREVER

Nothing lasts forever, and your starring role in your business will eventually come to an end. How you approach the end of your career will very much depend on your age and when and how you intend to depart, and also on whether you plan to head into retirement, start another business, or do something completely different.

It's all well and good building a successful company, but at some point you will want, or need, to liquidate your assets. You'll want to get out with a chunk of hard-earned money or dividend-earning shares. Being company rich and cash poor is to have all the responsibility and none of the fun. Even if you enjoy running your business, you may decide it's time to retire, or there is always the possibility you might become ill and need to liquidate your assets in a hurry. This, of course, is the worst position to be in if you expect to get a good price for your business. Early planning, therefore, can save a lot of headaches down the road.

You may not be in a position to do what I did, but I'll tell you the story of how I prepared my exit strategy almost forty years before I needed it. As with prenuptials, which are best negotiated before you get married (or shortly thereafter), exit strategies are best considered earlier rather than later.

When my company was only seven years old, I realized we were facing some serious issues, the biggest one being: How were we going to walk away from what we'd built? I had a business that consisted of a number of partners and franchisees. It wasn't one company; it was seventeen, and I owned a significant percentage of each one! None of my partners could afford to buy me out, and I couldn't afford to buy them out, so I asked myself the $64-million question (which would later become a $28-billion question): "Where's our liquidity?"

That's when I came up with the idea of consolidating into one company. My plan was to merge all seventeen partners and franchisees into one company. It took five years from the time I started bringing on board partners and franchisees until we amalgamated, but finally I consolidated the company. I have to admit, this process wasn't without its challenges, and the ensuing years were some of the toughest in my business career. But after we consolidated, we had a company we could take public and in which we could share ownership.

It is interesting to note that if the two people who had the least equity at the time of consolidation had retained all their shares, their individual stock today would be worth $250 million.

Managing Your Success

One of the keys to managing success is having a realistic understanding of how successful you are. I've seen too many situations where people start enterprises, they enjoy immediate success (or at least some level of success), and they start spending money. It's understandable that they want to enjoy the fruits of their labor, but they get way ahead of themselves and buy cars, houses, whatever. Of course, spouses are another major cause of concern. You may be managing and controlling your success, but what about your spouse? And what about your children; are they becoming spoiled?

Remember, especially in the early days, there are no guarantees as to how long your current level of success will last. Ask yourself, "Are my current revenues sustainable? Can I count on them?" Especially if you have just purchased a new house.

Some types of business are more dependable and consistent than others. Paychex, for instance, is a recurring revenue business, so it's consistent and predictable. With a business like that, once you achieve a level of success, you can with some degree of certainty expect that it's going to continue. That's the huge benefit of a recurring revenue business. But if you're in an industry or a business that has wild fluctuations, and during a successful period you over-enjoy your success, you could end up in a lot of trouble. One bit of advice I give to the entrepreneurs I work with about success is don't get a big head, because you never know when a business can turn on you.

Another inherent danger with success is a desire to gamble on new ventures. People often think, *I've been successful in this, so I can be successful in any venture I become involved in.* When an entrepreneur starts to believe his or her own press, danger lurks just around the next bend. One of my favorite sayings is, "You can fail many times, but you only have to be successful once. But once you're successful, don't ever bet the farm on a new venture or idea."

When Is It Time to Leave?

When to step down is completely up to you; there will be dozens of factors to take into consideration, ranging from how you feel about walking away and the potential value and salability of your company to the company's future sustainability.

Whatever your situation, at some stage you will need to ask yourself: "Is my long-term goal selling the business at some point, or will I stay until they wheel me out in a box?" and "Do I want someone in my family to take over the business?" We'll explore some of your options in this chapter, but for now, be honest. Do you from time to time ask yourself, "Geez, is it time to sell? I wonder what I might get for the company"? If you do, then perhaps you should do some strategic planning.

One thing I can guarantee is that it's never too early to start thinking about your exit strategy. I admit I didn't have an exit strategy from day one of Paychex, but I soon learned the necessity of planning for the day you want (or have) to step aside.

Before You Sell

If you start to seriously consider selling your business, be very careful about making any long-term commitments such as real estate leases or the purchase of equipment. These can get in the way of a successful sale. New owners may not agree with the commitments, or they may obstruct the direction in which the new owner may want to take the company.

As far as employees are concerned, it's best they are not aware of your intention to sell the company until much later in the sale process. It is natural for people to be apprehensive about the future of their jobs, and some may start seeking alternative employment. Although their fears may be understandable, they are often unfounded. Most acquirers will want key employees and senior management to remain under the new management; they may even offer incentive contracts to those people they see as integral to the company's well-being.

Selling Your Business

If you decide to sell your business, there are several ways you can approach the sale, but first you might want to consider when and why you should explore this option before you consider how you might approach finding a buyer.

Why Sell Your Business?

There are many reasons why you might decide to sell your business. You may have achieved all your goals and the business no longer challenges you. You may simply be bored, or you may have another business concept you would like to explore or invest in, or you might just decide now is the time to retire and spend more time with your family or on your hobbies.

There is no bad reason to sell your business, unless you are trying to unload it because it is experiencing major challenges.

Whatever your reason, spend some time considering what you will do after you sell. Many owners, especially those in their late forties and early fifties, sell and then find they are bored and miss the excitement of running a business. Of course, you can always start a new business or do what I did and start investing in up-and-coming businesses. A word of warning, though: if you sell and find you are drawn back into entrepreneurship, don't bet the farm. I've seen people who have built a successful business, sell it, do extremely well financially, only to lose it all in a new venture. This happened to at least four of my original Paychex colleagues and they still regret it to this day, especially when their wives mention that they should have stayed with payroll processing.

Knowing When to Sell the Business

Every circumstance is different. Sometimes you don't have the luxury of being able to sell at the perfect time, just when your business is doing well, and you are ready to step back.

Here's a story about how a little patience and persistence allowed us to sell at just the right moment.

I mentioned earlier that I had some serious issues with a company called Safe Site, where the controller of the company was kiting electronic cash transactions. As if dealing with the fallout of his actions weren't enough, our predicament became public and our national competitor, Iron Mountain, approached us and tried to take advantage of our embarrassing situation. They offered us $14 million. We discussed this low offer at a board meeting, and I was told that if we didn't accept their offer, we needed to find over $3 million in new capital. Everyone looked at me. If we were going to save the company, I'd have to come up with the money. I decided the time wasn't right to sell—it's never a good time to sell when you're on the back foot. I increased my equity position and left Iron Mountain very disappointed. From that point, we started to climb our own mountain back to profitability.

A couple of years later I was attending an investment conference and an analyst friend approached me and asked whether we were interested in selling. It turned out the inquiry was from a company called Pierce Leahy. We entered into discussions, and they subsequently offered us $40 million. Not a bad hike from Iron Mountain's offer of $14 million just a year or two before. I ran it by my principal partner, and he felt if we went back to Iron Mountain they would pay more.

I contacted them and negotiated a price of $63 million. In just a few years we went from close to bankruptcy to financial success.

This is an object lesson in perseverance and knowing the right time to sell. Often you need to stick it out if you're convinced it's a good idea and the company will succeed over the long haul. Of course, as this situation also demonstrates, painfully, you need to be fully aware of your financial situation at all times. Not just to understand the basic financial statements, although they are vitally important, but to ensure there are sufficient checks and balances on anyone dealing with the company's finances.

Turning the Business Over to an Heir

This can be a tough decision. It can also be fraught with danger. Before considering this option, be sure the business has a long-term future, that it is sustainable. Ask yourself if there are any new and improved products or services coming out that will affect your market. What about new technology? How might that impact your business? Will it require extensive investment or make what you sell obsolete?

It's always tempting to believe, or wish, that your children or grand-children have the ability to take on your business and even potentially take it to new heights. You need to be honest with yourself. Do they have the skills, experience, and business acumen to keep your business growing? And how much of your time and help are you willing to give them to teach them how to be successful in the business?

How Will You Sell?

If your company is doing well and you have a high profile, the like-lihood is that at some point one of your competitors will knock on your door and make you an offer. Over the years Paychex bought companies for their software, for their customer lists, and for many other reasons.

If your thoughts turn toward selling, even if you are not immediately considering it, begin thinking about what an attractive but realistic price might be. What is the lowest reasonable amount that would still make you sit up and take notice? Too often business owners put a ridiculously high price on their company and they are never able to sell. If selling is even a possibility in your mind, it might be a good idea to get your business appraised.

In chapter 3, I discussed the importance of understanding financial statements; now is the time to ensure that all your financial information is up to date. A well-planned sale is likely to result in a far higher sale price than one where you suddenly and arbitrarily decide it's time to sell. There are a lot of books available on the topic of succession planning, and these might be useful as a guide to how you should approach handing your business over to a new owner, whether that's your grandchild or a competitor.

There are also companies or individual brokers who will sell your business for you; think of them like Realtors, but instead of selling your house, they are selling your business. Choose your broker wisely and interview several before making a decision. And don't fall into the trap of hiring the one who says he or she can get the highest price for your business. Starting out too high can mean months and months of inaction; this can make it look like your business is not desirable. A realistic price will attract more than one suitor, which will put you in a better position to negotiate terms.

Businesses don't sell overnight, and a sale can take several years to work its way through the many stages of due diligence toward an eventual change of ownership. Be patient.

How Will You Get Paid?

This may seem a strange question, but unlike selling a house, where you can expect the purchaser to simply pay the going price on the day you close the deal, acquirers of businesses can be considerably more creative in how they offer to pay for your company.

The best scenario is you receive the asking price in cash with no strings attached. They pay, you walk, all good. Second best: they pay cash, but you don't walk, well, at least not immediately. You hang around in a consultative role during a transition period, during which you may be able to negotiate some sort of "salary" or payment of some description.

Another option if your company is being purchased by a public company is to be paid with a mix of cash and stock. This, of course, can be a gamble, depending on the company making the purchase. If the company is doing well, then it might be worth the risk, but you will need to carry out some significant due diligence. If the company continues to do well and you hang on to the shares, you could end up with a substantial gain on the original sale. As I said, it's a gamble; only you can decide whether the odds are in your favor.

Some acquirers will ask you, at least in part, to fund the sale. They may offer you 20 to 30 percent down and then plan to pay the rest over time. I would be very cautious about such deals. Often under new management, companies can experience a downturn in sales and profits. This can occur for many reasons; perhaps key employees or senior management staff decide to leave, or the new people are not as experienced or as effective in running the company as you were. Whatever the reason, if the company is not doing well, you will not be one of the first people they pay, believe me.

This type of deal is often used when handing the business over to family members, but there lies a future fraught with potential difficulty. I would only suggest contemplating this if you are convinced the person or persons involved have the capacity to make the business a continuing success. In these cases, you have to be hard-nosed and put familial allegiance and love to one side—this is business, and no one wins if the business fails.

Stepping Down and Stepping Up

One of the challenges you will face when you sell your business is that the acquirer will likely request that you stay on for anywhere from six months to five years until they get well adjusted to their acquisition. In many cases owners agree to this and then later have issues with the new owners and leave anyway. This can lead to a "so sue me" situation, which can be unpleasant for all parties. This is another reason to plan your exit from the business well in advance. If you leave too late, those "extra" few years can seem very long, especially if you were planning to buy a boat and sail off into the sunset.

Whatever course of action you decide to take, the biggest advice I can give you is once you have decided to sell the company and you have settled on a price and the terms of the sale, don't spend any more time thinking about it—don't look back. Enjoy what you've got; don't continually chew on it, or it'll drive you crazy.

You've Sold—You're Free!

You've sold, you're free! What do you do now that you are cash rich and have a large hole in your life where your business used to be? Success affects different people in different ways. I've seen it all. This is not the time to immediately jump into something new. Take some time to evaluate your life and decide what you miss about owning your own business and what you are glad to leave behind. Several of my partners in Paychex decided to cut and run in the early days because they thought they could replicate their success in another industry. Some did okay, but others regret their decision to this day, and they check Paychex's stock daily to see what they might have been worth had they stuck it out. That's sad. "Never get ahead of yourself" is solid advice.

For my part, when I retired, I decided to invest in up-and-coming businesses where my expertise and experience might be useful. I currently work with twelve businesses, and they keep me busy enough and I'd like to say out of trouble, but hey, this is the world of business and there are no certainties.

Forget the Stock Options—I'll Take My Credenza

If selling your business does not appeal to you, there is always the option of stepping back and putting someone else in charge of running the business. I stepped down as CEO of Paychex fourteen years ago, but I still own a percentage of the company and I'm chairman of the board. I no longer have any day-to-day responsibilities, but I have the comfort of being able to keep watch over the company while receiving annual dividends on my stock. This can seem to offer the best of both worlds, but it may not be for everyone.

Before I left, one of the concerns the new CEO raised in the interview process was that as I not only was the founder of Paychex but had been running it for over thirty years, I would be tempted to interfere with the way he might choose to run the company. It was a concern I could understand and relate to, so from the day I walked out of the office for the final time as CEO, I didn't return for three months except to deal with a legal issue that specifically required my attendance. I did, however, have to return for a brief spell when our initial choice for CEO didn't work out and we needed to hire someone different; that person, Marty Mucci, is CEO to this day. Even though I am still, as I mentioned, chairman of the board, I do not have an office in Paychex's corporate headquarters.

My earlier advice about not looking back after selling your business also goes for stepping back from your business after putting someone else in charge. Choose well and leave them to run the business with minimal input, and only then when absolutely necessary.

The circumstances surrounding my retirement have surprised many business pundits, and they reflect my somewhat contrary philosophy about the corporate world. As I said previously, I've always thought that CEOs of US companies are paid too highly. My own salary was lower in comparison to most heads of similar-size companies. Not only that, my total remuneration package was also significantly lower. When one looks at a CEO's salary, it only shows a fraction of their true compensation package—there are bonuses and stock options to include before arriving at the full amount. Too often CEOs and senior management enjoy salaries that are not linked to their company's performance. I believe those running a company should only do well when the corporation is doing well.

When I finally stepped down as CEO of Paychex, I didn't have a golden parachute and I took no stock options, even though they were offered. My retirement package was my desk and my credenza, two items I treasured.

Earlier I recommended you not look back on the sale of your company, and I'll add to that not to look back at prior deals you made and wonder whether they were the right or wrong things to do. But I have to admit I have taken one or two looks back at my previous business life, though from a positive perspective.

I recently attended a staff appreciation picnic and was touched by the number of people who came up to say hi, the number of people who wanted a selfie, and those new to the firm who wanted to meet me and shake my hand.

One of the most memorable moments of my postretirement life

was addressing Paychex employees at the 2016 Employee Meeting. Marty asked me to be a surprise guest, and I was blown away by the reception I received. Over four thousand employees applauded when I stepped on stage, and at the end of my speech the standing ovation was overwhelming.

After the event I spent two hours taking selfies with Paychex's wonderful employees. It's not often that the founder of a company remains as CEO for thirty-three years, and I think that sets me apart from many of today's corporate leaders. I have a relationship with Paychex that is unique in the depth of its intimacy—a strange word perhaps when talking about a company, but fitting in this case, I think.

Running a company such as Paychex was a privilege, and I owe my success to the many dedicated people who worked alongside me over the years, not to mention our loyal customers.

In the final analysis, I achieved my aim of eventual liquidity and a sound exit strategy—and so can you.

Takeaways

- Ask yourself, "How am I going to walk away from what I've built?"
- There are three primary options when thinking of an exit strategy from your business: sell it, pass it to a family member, or run it passively.
- Exit strategies are best considered sooner than later.
- Ensure you have a realistic understanding of your current level of success.

- Constantly question the sustainability of your current revenue level. Never get ahead of yourself.
- Understand how stable your industry and business are and what could detrimentally affect that stability.
- Avoid long-term commitments you may not be able to maintain or that might hamper selling your business.
- Ensure your spouse has the same level of understanding and is not overspending.
- Don't spoil your children just because you finally have the means to do so.
- Wait patiently for the right time to sell, and don't sell too early.
- Don't invest more than you can easily afford to lose in your own business or another venture.

ELEVEN

REGRETS, I'VE HAD A FEW

During my long career as an entrepreneur, I've learned more from watching people fail than succeed. I'm always interested in seeing what went wrong in a business and then figuring out a way to avoid that particular mistake. I'm certainly not immune to making mistakes; over the years I have regretted several decisions I either made or failed to make in businesses I owned or invested in, and each one made me a stronger and better entrepreneur. Let me share a few examples.

Too Many Players

My first regret dates back to the early days of Paychex, in the 1970s. As I mentioned before, when I first started the company, I had no intention of making it a national business, but people started approaching me and I began taking on partners and selling franchises. Looking back, I think I would have been better to have capped the number at around ten, but I had difficulty saying no to people who offered to move to a new city and start a new Paychex branch.

My big regret is that I didn't really have a plan. The company grew territory by territory when people came along and convinced me they could make a success of launching a new office. If my criteria for choosing partners and franchisees had been stricter and I had brought fewer people on board, I think it's likely that the company would have grown faster and today my share of the company would be greater. Having seventeen people reporting to me was a headache of epic proportions. I remember one occasion where we spent the better part of a day discussing whether the company should pay for employees' coffee.

Now, having said that, I have nothing against any of my old partners. They were all good people; they worked hard and did a good job. But a little strategic planning in those very early days would have paid dividends (literally) later. The moral of this story is to avoid letting things happen; take planning seriously.

Not Bringing EAS on Board

I'll always regret not being able to convince Electronic Accounting Systems to join forces with me. Even before I launched the forerunner of Paychex, Paymaster, I'd tried to convince the company of the potential of selling payroll processing services to small businesses, but I never could persuade them of the massive value of the market. Several years later, when Paychex was preparing to go public, I once again offered them an opportunity to be part of the public offering and once again the CEO turned down the offer.

Even though we ended up being competitors, I was friends with a lot of the people in the company and had strong relationships with them. Some years later, EAS was sold, but for a tiny fraction of what they would have been worth had they taken me up on my offer of joining Paychex. That's a huge regret for me, but I'm not sure what else I could have done to convince them.

Looking back at other regrets I can almost track the way I learned how to be a successful entrepreneur: how to make money, not lose it; how to focus on what is important; and how to spot a good opportunity rather than just a shiny one.

A Monster Mistake

Shortly after Paychex went public, I made a serious mistake. We had acquired another company, and the management team had been working on an idea to match employers with job seekers. This idea was similar to the concept of the highly successful www.monster.com. It was a good idea, but to provide a matchmaking service of this kind in the mid-1970s, long before the internet existed, was expensive and cumbersome. Once the internet arrived, www.monster.com showed us all what a great idea it had been with access to the right technology.

My timing could not have been worse. With Paychex having only recently gone public, Wall Street was watching us closely, and they began asking with considerable disdain, "What are you doing with this venture?" They saw this new company as way beyond our normal business parameters, and it made them very uncomfortable. As a result, the company only lasted about ten months before I pulled the plug and shut it down.

During that period, we lost credibility with Wall Street at a time when we should have been consolidating our relationship. I learned through that experience not to enter a business where the market isn't ready for the service you want to provide, that's outside your area of expertise, or where current technology cannot meet the distribution needs of what you are selling. My regret is that I broke my own rules when I let others convince me of the validity of a concept that went counter to my gut instincts.

I Paid to Play

I'm known for my sound investments, and in recent years, for the most part, they have been highly successful, but I have several regrets over situations where I got it all wrong. One such business was Pay to Play. The idea was simple: We had facilities in shopping malls full of games for children. Parents could rent the space for birthday parties, and we'd supply cake and other refreshments. We lasted a year, and I lost $500,000. As the primary investor, I took a significant hit. This was a case of not having a business plan that demonstrated exactly how we could make enough money to pay the bills. My advice is that if you fail to develop a good business plan, you, like me, will regret it; in this case to the tune of half a million dollars.

Not Keeping My Poise

Another one of my early ventures from thirty-plus years ago was a business called Equipoise. My regret with that particular business is that I invested in a concept that was out of my normal comfort zone. I didn't even know what the word *equipoise* meant at first, but I soon learned that it referred to a balance between lifestyles that makes a person comfortable and happy in their skin.

Louise Woerner, the founder of Health Care Resources Consulting Group (HCR), approached me with the idea of starting an alternative and complementary health-care facility where practitioners could rent space in the center and pay a percentage of their sales revenue to Equipoise. The concept behind Equipoise was strong in that it made sense to bring together chiropractic, acupuncture, acupressure, aromatherapy, biofeedback, massage therapy, reflexology, and other medicines in one place at one time. HCR was and still is a highly successful operation, and Louise had a stellar business background. Her business credentials included CEO and chairperson of HealthNow New York Inc. and a director of First Niagara Bank, National Association.

I was attracted to the business because I'd had some personal experience with acupuncture. At that time, I'd been a smoker for twenty-seven years and after just one hour of treatment I walked out of the acupuncturist's office and never had a desire to smoke again. I remember I kept a pack of cigarettes in the console of my car for a week and a carton at home and finally gave them away. I'd also used acupuncture to treat my baseball-throwing arm for several years, so the concept of alternative medicine impressed me.

I was a believer, but you need more than blind belief in something for it to be successful. I did, however, have a good partner and a concept I thought should succeed, but we never had a well-thought-out business plan and we didn't carry out enough market research. This was back in the 1980s in Rochester, New York. In retrospect, the concept was way ahead of its time and in the end never managed to generate sufficient revenues from practitioners' rents to get it off the ground.

Hanging In for Too Long

Then there was Networks, a business that was close to my heart, and my regret was having to close it down when it was still servicing a small but loyal group of listeners. Networks offered specialized music programming in senior residences and nursing homes. I started it because my partner and I owned some broadcasting equipment from another business that failed, but that's another story. The idea was to broadcast music that came from the era the residents had lived through, music they would relate to and enjoy. This was once again a recurring revenue opportunity; we charged a fee per bed, per month.

The business got off to a good start, but we continually struggled to cover our overhead, due to the high cost of installing the equipment. We managed to build it to a point where we were broadcasting in three hundred residences, but the added high cost of sales was killing us. The challenge we faced was a long selling cycle to the nursing homes, as they operated on tight margins and had significant budgetary constraints, combined with the fact that sales representatives had to travel long distances between prospects.

I kept that business going for many years past its sell-by date for sentimental reasons, but in 2017, after investing over $12 million, we had to close it down. For one thing, technology was against us; even older seniors owned smartphones and tablets that could stream music. We couldn't even sell the business to another operator.

Hiring the Wrong Person

I've not had many human resource regrets and have usually been satisfied with my hiring and firing decisions. There is, however, one exception, and that was when we needed to hire my replacement when I retired as CEO from Paychex. The person we hired went through an extensive interviewing process; he had excellent credentials, the right background, good references, and a strong interview. The rest of my board felt good about him, but my gut instinct was that he just wasn't the right person for the job. In the end, he wasn't a good fit, and after five years he left. His replacement, Marty Mucci, has been CEO for eight years now and has done an excellent job for the company; I consider him one of my best hires. But to this day I regret not following my instincts and hiring the wrong person initially.

Missing Family

A common regret I am sure I share with many entrepreneurs is not spending as much time with my family as I should have. This is a tough one because you are working hard building your company so that you can provide a better standard of living for your spouse and children. However, I do regret not finding a better balance. Work-life balance has become a big thing in business in recent years, and I'm not sure how qualified I am in giving advice on the subject, but remember it's no good being successful and having no one with whom to share that success.

Takeaways

- You can often learn more from people in business who fail than from those who succeed.
- Have a plan; don't let your business just evolve.
- A little strategic planning can pay dividends.
- Focus on what's important rather than shiny.
- Never let others convince you of the validity of a concept that goes counter to your gut instinct.

BUILT, NOT BORN

- Do sufficient research to ensure your business concept is not ahead of its time.
- Don't hang in too long for the wrong reasons.
- Remember how important your family is to you.

TWELVE

WHAT CAN WE ALL DO BETTER?

Throughout this book I've offered what I see as basic, no-nonsense advice on running and managing a business. There is a lot you as a businessperson can do to increase the likelihood that your business will be successful, but what about all those organizations that either hinder your growth at worst or are ineffective in helping you grow your business at best? In this chapter I'll also talk about some organizations that can be beneficial to you and your company.

Entrepreneurship is the backbone of the American economy; however, there are many sectors of society that fail to recognize this and that could do far more to support the small business community. I'm talking about educational institutions, the federal government, local state government, the media, and even business associations such as chambers of commerce.

Did you know that America's 30.2 million small businesses employ 58.9 million people? According to the latest Small Business Profile published by the US Small Business Administration, 99 percent of businesses in the United States are small businesses. And of course, these are run by entrepreneurs. In 2015, the small business community added 1.9 million jobs; 1.1 million of those people were hired by companies with fewer than twenty employees.[2] Small business is the growth engine of the United States, yet it is a sector that is overregulated, is ignored, and gets little true support from the very organizations that should be providing assistance, or at least not getting in the way of growth.

Education

I believe entrepreneurship is so important to the American economy that our educational system should teach and promote it as part of secondary school curriculum. When I say this, some people look surprised; it's as if this is a strange thing to suggest. But to me teaching young people about business is no different from teaching art, music, and foreign languages, the latter of which is sometimes mandatory. Others claim that not every young person is going to leave school and start a business, and they are correct. But a very large percentage *will* go out into the business world and hope to find a job.

Now, answer me this: Given the small business statistics provided above, how many of these young people are going to be looking for a job with a *small* business? A large percentage, of course, so here's another question: If you are a small business owner interviewing a young person straight from school, would you prefer them to be able to play the French horn, tell you why Van Gogh cut off his ear, or have a fundamental understanding of how the American capitalist system works and have been taught to read financial statements, understand basic accounting principles, know how marketing works, have some salesmanship skills, know common government regulations, and possess other knowledge that will help you immediately grow your business? Of course, if you'd like them to play you Mozart's Horn Concerto no. 1, choose the former.

Don't get me wrong. I'm not saying that learning about art, music, and especially a language such as Spanish isn't useful. I just feel that it's even more important for our young people to gain a fundamental understanding of how the American economy works and have the necessary knowledge to help them either launch their own enterprise or get good jobs and hopefully become entrepreneurial employees.

Here's another thought: Did you know that more than half of the families in the United States own stocks or equities in various companies, but few understand the financial statements put out by these corporations and investment funds? To me that is a basic skill everyone should learn at school; that and balancing a checking account.

Our educational system needs to move ahead fifty or sixty years; the age of cradle-to-grave jobs is long gone, as are many of the companies that used to provide those jobs. Even those that have survived, such as U.S. Steel, are shadows of their former selves. It is time to celebrate entrepreneurship, build enthusiasm around it, and recognize its value to the future of our people and our country—for those looking to start their own business, those who own businesses, and those who want to work in or manage a business. Schools have a real opportunity to create an environment of success for entrepreneurism by giving students the skills they need to survive in the real world—the world of business. This poses the question: Is the educational system even up to the challenge?

Government in All Its Guises

If you own a business in the United States, you have a not-so-silent partner in your business that puts up no capital, shares none of the risk with you, but expects to regularly take a significant percentage of your hard-earned profits. All this, while at the same time making your business life a whole lot more difficult than it needs to be. That partner, of course, is the federal government.

While the government is absent when it comes to helping out with financing your business or offsetting some of the risk, it's not so silent when it comes to telling you how to run your business. Your silent partner will tell you how your employees should be paid, what kind of fringe benefits you have to offer, what hours and overtime rules you have to follow, and which safety regulations must be enforced in your business, such as those regulated by OSHA (Occupational Safety and Health Administration). As partners go, they are like the third wheel on a first date.

Much of this also applies to state or local government. Most states have their own set of rules relative to minimum wage, hours worked, fringe benefits, and more, all of which must be followed. Where the state really gets involved is in the area of workers' compensation insurance, disability insurance, unemployment insurance, and family leave. These are all significant financial burdens to employers.

In addition, local governments add another set of burdens on business owners, such as zoning restrictions, building permits, and high local taxes, and they very often create expensive and frustrating delays in getting businesses established due to licensing and other administrative red tape. I was involved with one business in Florida where it took us almost four months to build and open a small 1,200-square-foot location. In New York State, to its benefit, we can set up the same business in about three weeks.

My point here is that a lot depends on where your business is located; one state can make certain things easy; in another they can be burdensome. Some state regulations can be pro-business, and in others they can hinder your business's operation. Navigating a state's protocols can be a nightmare, only to discover federal regulations over-lay those of each state.

Government always seems to make business complex and difficult. I would like to see all levels of government keep their business rules and regulations to a minimum. This would greatly help small businesses function more effectively, efficiently, and profitably. Even though the administrative and tax burdens various levels of government put in place are, in their mind anyway, well intended, they can be a significant burden on small businesses. And some are downright unnecessary, such as when the federal government introduced a few years ago a requirement that companies have to report hiring a new employee within thirty days of their starting with the company.

I have several other issues with state governments, including their desire to create jobs using government subsidies. In my opinion this is a rifle approach rather than a shotgun approach because these states provide funds to only a limited number of organizations or companies. The hope is that these fortunate companies will create more jobs, but there are no guarantees this will occur; in fact, there have been many cases of start-up companies using state money that haven't created the jobs they predicted.

In some cases, the amount of funding is so great that the return on investment on this taxpayer-funded activity could never show a return on investment in terms of tax income to the government. I've seen grants amounting to $100,000 an employee. Now, how many years in the state of New York, at the rate state employees pay income tax, would it take for them to get the money back? I'll tell you: decades!

Far more jobs would be created by lowering taxes for everyone, but perhaps that's too simple a solution for governments who often feel a need to overcomplicate everything.

One of the reasons for what I see as a misuse of taxpayer money is that almost all states are funding this type of job creation; therefore, any state that opts out believes it will be at a disadvantage. The federal government could step in and stop the practice, but I doubt they are inclined to do so for fear of interfering with what is seen as a state-level issue. At the end of the day, taxpayer money is being wasted, as usual.

Another misguided policy enacted by most, if not all, states is financial assistance given to companies offering to locate or relocate their operations to a specific state. Companies will often pitch state against state with this carrot, hoping the subsidies will rise as the competition for the jobs they will provide heats up. CEOs are trained to do this; in fact, you might say they are obligated to do it to benefit their shareholders. Amazon has shown itself particularly proficient at what is a race to the bottom for the states involved.

As I mentioned previously, I used to own the Buffalo Sabres, and so have some experience in that arena (sorry, but that pun was intended) when it comes to state-sponsored funding. State government politicians are so frightened of losing a sports team franchise that they will do almost anything to appease the sports team owner or the league that wants a new stadium or arena. And that includes spending millions of dollars of taxpayer money. It reminds me of the days of the Colosseum in Rome, when the emperor provided entertainment to all citizens by building a stadium.

Media

In my experience, the media sometimes has a tendency to belittle or berate businesses that experience notable success. The approach they take when covering success stories can often give the reader the impression that there was something unethical, underhand, or even illegal taking place to warrant such an achievement. It seems the media's default is to put entrepreneurs down and cast a shadow over their successes. This is detrimental to the American psyche. Business and entrepreneurship are important to the future of the United States, and the media can do a lot more to support the growth of small businesses. More emphasis should be put on the fact that successful organizations create jobs; these companies invest the capital to build new factories, purchase new equipment, and create new services.

I believe that embracing and celebrating successful entrepreneurs and their businesses is good for the American people and the economy. I would like to read more well-researched, accurate articles highlighting entrepreneurial success.

Business Associations

The Small Business Trends website lists twenty-eight business associations on its "The Really Big List of Small Business Associations,"[3] so there is no shortage of organizations you can turn to for support. I've always thought that unless the annual dues are going to cause you hardship or you believe they do not reflect the value you will receive, it's a good idea to belong to whatever business associations are active in your community.

There are more than four thousand chambers of commerce across the United States that employ at least one full-time person and thousands of smaller operations run by volunteers from the business community. Checking in with your local chamber is probably a good place to start. From a national perspective, the US Chamber of Commerce is the world's largest business organization. It represents the interests of more than three million businesses and local chambers across the country. It is the voice of business in Washington, DC.

Other notable associations from the "really big list" include the three-hundred-thousand-strong National Federation for Independent Businesses (NFIB); the National Business Association; Business Network International (BNI), which can often have multiple groups in one town or city; and many specialist organizations such as the International Franchise Association and the National Restaurant Association. My advice is to do a little research and discover which associations are more likely to be useful to you and have members with whom you would be interested in networking.

Becoming active in associations like these gets your name out in the community, along with your company's profile. That is always a positive, especially in terms of being able to promote your products and services. Mixing with other businesspeople can also be a valuable learning experience. A side benefit of attending mixers and functions is that you might come across recruitment opportunities, both in terms of general employees and senior management.

This type of networking will inevitably put you in the same room, from time to time, with your competition; I suggest never underestimating the potential of building positive relationships and alliances with your competitors. It has worked well for me over the years.

One final benefit of being heavily involved in your local business community is getting to know what issues are affecting, or might affect, the local business community in general, or your particular industry.

A Final Word

I hope you have enjoyed this book. Writing it has been a labor of love. Hopefully you have learned a little about the ins and outs, and maybe the machinations, of running a business; the things to watch for, the things to avoid, the things to embrace. I have enjoyed my business career greatly. Watching Paychex grow from just myself, one employee, $3,000, and a well-worn credit card to a company employing 15,500 people servicing 670,000 clients has been amazing fun and a genuine privilege.

I believe entrepreneurs are extremely important to our country and to our future. I have the utmost respect for the people who take the risk to become an entrepreneur and the value they can and do create for our citizens. They should be honored and celebrated, and yes, I'm talking about people like you.

If I can pass on one more piece of sage wisdom: "Don't forget to have fun!"

Takeaways

- Small business is the growth engine of the United States.
- America's 30.2 million small businesses employ 58.9 million people.
- Ninety-nine percent of businesses in the United States are small businesses.
- In 2015, the small business community added 1.9 million jobs; 1.1 million of those people were hired by companies with fewer than twenty employees.
- The US educational system needs to move ahead fifty or sixty years; the age of cradle-to-grave jobs is long gone, as are many of the companies that used to provide those jobs.
- The school system should teach entrepreneurial studies.
- More than half of the families in the United States own

stocks or equities in various companies, but few understand the financial statements put out by these corporations and investment funds.

- The federal government is your silent partner in business.
- Embracing and celebrating successful entrepreneurs and their businesses is good for the American people and the economy. We need media to publish more well-researched, accurate articles highlighting entrepreneurial success.
- It's beneficial to belong to whatever business associations are active in your community.
- Don't forget to have fun!

NOTES

1. US Small Business Administration Office of Advocacy, *2018 Small Business Profile*, accessed April 11, 2019, https://www.sba.gov/sites /default/files/advocacy/2018-Small-Business-Profiles-US.pdf.
2. US Small Business Administration.
3. Annie Pilon, "The Really Big List of Small Business Associations," May 16, 2018, Small Business Trends, https://smallbiztrends.com/2018/05 /small-business-associations.html.